ISBN 0-8373-0848-8
C-848   CAREER EXAMINATION SERIES

This is your PASSBOOK® for...

Budget Assistant

Test Preparation Study Guide

Questions & Answers

NLC
NATIONAL LEARNING CORPORATION

Copyright © 2015 by

National Learning Corporation

212 Michael Drive, Syosset, New York 11791

All rights reserved, including the right of reproduction in whole or in part, in any form or by any means, electronic or mechanical, including photocopying, recording, or by any information storage and retrieval system, without permission in writing from the Publisher.

(516) 921-8888
(800) 645-6337
FAX: (516) 921-8743
www.passbooks.com
sales @ passbooks.com
info @ passbooks.com

PRINTED IN THE UNITED STATES OF AMERICA

PASSBOOK®
NOTICE

This book is SOLELY intended for, is sold ONLY to, and its use is RESTRICTED to *individual*, bona fide applicants or candidates who qualify by virtue of having seriously filed applications for appropriate license, certificate, professional and/or promotional advancement, higher school matriculation, scholarship, or other legitimate requirements of educational and/or governmental authorities.

This book is NOT intended for use, class instruction, tutoring, training, duplication, copying, reprinting, excerption, or adaptation, etc., by:

(1) Other publishers

(2) Proprietors and/or Instructors of "Coaching" and/or Preparatory Courses

(3) Personnel and/or Training Divisions of commercial, industrial, and governmental organizations

(4) Schools, colleges, or universities and/or their departments and staffs, including teachers and other personnel

(5) Testing Agencies or Bureaus

(6) Study groups which seek by the purchase of a single volume to copy and/or duplicate and/or adapt this material for use by the group as a whole without having purchased individual volumes for each of the members of the group

(7) Et al.

Such persons would be in violation of appropriate Federal and State statutes.

PROVISION OF LICENSING AGREEMENTS. — Recognized educational commercial, industrial, and governmental institutions and organizations, and others legitimately engaged in educational pursuits, including training, testing, and measurement activities, may address a request for a licensing agreement to the copyright owners, who will determine whether, and under what conditions, including fees and charges, the materials in this book may be used by them. In other words, a licensing facility exists for the legitimate use of the material in this book on other than an individual basis. However, it is asseverated and affirmed here that the material in this book *CANNOT* be used without the receipt of the express permission of such a licensing agreement from the Publishers.

NATIONAL LEARNING CORPORATION
212 Michael Drive
Syosset, New York 11791

Inquiries re licensing agreements should be addressed to:
The President
National Learning Corporation
212 Michael Drive
Syosset, New York 11791

PASSBOOK® SERIES

THE *PASSBOOK® SERIES* has been created to prepare applicants and candidates for the ultimate academic battlefield — the examination room.

At some time in our lives, each and every one of us may be required to take an examination — for validation, matriculation, admission, qualification, registration, certification, or licensure.

Based on the assumption that every applicant or candidate has met the basic formal educational standards, has taken the required number of courses, and read the necessary texts, the *PASSBOOK® SERIES* furnishes the one special preparation which may assure passing with confidence, instead of failing with insecurity. Examination questions — together with answers — are furnished as the basic vehicle for study so that the mysteries of the examination and its compounding difficulties may be eliminated or diminished by a sure method.

This book is meant to help you pass your examination provided that you qualify and are serious in your objective.

The entire field is reviewed through the huge store of content information which is succinctly presented through a provocative and challenging approach — the question-and-answer method.

A climate of success is established by furnishing the correct answers at the end of each test.

You soon learn to recognize types of questions, forms of questions, and patterns of questioning. You may even begin to anticipate expected outcomes.

You perceive that many questions are repeated or adapted so that you can gain acute insights, which may enable you to score many sure points.

You learn how to confront new questions, or types of questions, and to attack them confidently and work out the correct answers.

You note objectives and emphases, and recognize pitfalls and dangers, so that you may make positive educational adjustments.

Moreover, you are kept fully informed in relation to new concepts, methods, practices, and directions in the field.

You discover that you are actually taking the examination all the time: you are preparing for the examination by "taking" an examination, not by reading extraneous and/or supererogatory textbooks.

In short, this PASSBOOK®, used directedly, should be an important factor in helping you to pass your test.

BUDGET ASSISTANT

DUTIES

An employee in this class assists budget office staff with the preparation, authorization and execution phases of the budgetary process for the capital and operating budgets. The incumbent is expected to complete tasks requiring specialized knowledge of budgetary techniques, administration and processes independently, but refers the more difficult technical decisions to supervisory personnel. The work involves responsibility for performing highly specialized work related to the preparation, production and execution of a municipality's operating and capital budgets. Work is performed under the general supervision of an assigned technical or administrative supervisor and is reviewed while in progress and upon completion for the achievement of desired results. Does related work as required.

SCOPE OF THE EXAMINATION

The written test will cover knowledge, skills, and/or abilities in such areas as:
1. Arithmetic computation with calculator;
2. Coding/decoding information;
3. Office record keeping;
4. Organizing data into tables and records; and
5. Understanding and interpreting written material.

HOW TO TAKE A TEST

I. YOU MUST PASS AN EXAMINATION

A. *WHAT EVERY CANDIDATE SHOULD KNOW*

Examination applicants often ask us for help in preparing for the written test. What can I study in advance? What kinds of questions will be asked? How will the test be given? How will the papers be graded?

As an applicant for a civil service examination, you may be wondering about some of these things. Our purpose here is to suggest effective methods of advance study and to describe civil service examinations.

Your chances for success on this examination can be increased if you know how to prepare. Those "pre-examination jitters" can be reduced if you know what to expect. You can even experience an adventure in good citizenship if you know why civil service exams are given.

B. *WHY ARE CIVIL SERVICE EXAMINATIONS GIVEN?*

Civil service examinations are important to you in two ways. As a citizen, you want public jobs filled by employees who know how to do their work. As a job seeker, you want a fair chance to compete for that job on an equal footing with other candidates. The best-known means of accomplishing this two-fold goal is the competitive examination.

Exams are widely publicized throughout the nation. They may be administered for jobs in federal, state, city, municipal, town or village governments or agencies.

Any citizen may apply, with some limitations, such as the age or residence of applicants. Your experience and education may be reviewed to see whether you meet the requirements for the particular examination. When these requirements exist, they are reasonable and applied consistently to all applicants. Thus, a competitive examination may cause you some uneasiness now, but it is your privilege and safeguard.

C. *HOW ARE CIVIL SERVICE EXAMS DEVELOPED?*

Examinations are carefully written by trained technicians who are specialists in the field known as "psychological measurement," in consultation with recognized authorities in the field of work that the test will cover. These experts recommend the subject matter areas or skills to be tested; only those knowledges or skills important to your success on the job are included. The most reliable books and source materials available are used as references. Together, the experts and technicians judge the difficulty level of the questions.

Test technicians know how to phrase questions so that the problem is clearly stated. Their ethics do not permit "trick" or "catch" questions. Questions may have been tried out on sample groups, or subjected to statistical analysis, to determine their usefulness.

Written tests are often used in combination with performance tests, ratings of training and experience, and oral interviews. All of these measures combine to form the best-known means of finding the right person for the right job.

II. HOW TO PASS THE WRITTEN TEST

A. NATURE OF THE EXAMINATION

To prepare intelligently for civil service examinations, you should know how they differ from school examinations you have taken. In school you were assigned certain definite pages to read or subjects to cover. The examination questions were quite detailed and usually emphasized memory. Civil service exams, on the other hand, try to discover your present ability to perform the duties of a position, plus your potentiality to learn these duties. In other words, a civil service exam attempts to predict how successful you will be. Questions cover such a broad area that they cannot be as minute and detailed as school exam questions.

In the public service similar kinds of work, or positions, are grouped together in one "class." This process is known as *position-classification*. All the positions in a class are paid according to the salary range for that class. One class title covers all of these positions, and they are all tested by the same examination.

B. FOUR BASIC STEPS

1) Study the announcement

How, then, can you know what subjects to study? Our best answer is: "Learn as much as possible about the class of positions for which you've applied." The exam will test the knowledge, skills and abilities needed to do the work.

Your most valuable source of information about the position you want is the official exam announcement. This announcement lists the training and experience qualifications. Check these standards and apply only if you come reasonably close to meeting them.

The brief description of the position in the examination announcement offers some clues to the subjects which will be tested. Think about the job itself. Review the duties in your mind. Can you perform them, or are there some in which you are rusty? Fill in the blank spots in your preparation.

Many jurisdictions preview the written test in the exam announcement by including a section called "Knowledge and Abilities Required," "Scope of the Examination," or some similar heading. Here you will find out specifically what fields will be tested.

2) Review your own background

Once you learn in general what the position is all about, and what you need to know to do the work, ask yourself which subjects you already know fairly well and which need improvement. You may wonder whether to concentrate on improving your strong areas or on building some background in your fields of weakness. When the announcement has specified "some knowledge" or "considerable knowledge," or has used adjectives like "beginning principles of..." or "advanced ... methods," you can get a clue as to the number and difficulty of questions to be asked in any given field. More questions, and hence broader coverage, would be included for those subjects which are more important in the work. Now weigh your strengths and weaknesses against the job requirements and prepare accordingly.

3) Determine the level of the position

Another way to tell how intensively you should prepare is to understand the level of the job for which you are applying. Is it the entering level? In other words, is this the position in which beginners in a field of work are hired? Or is it an intermediate or advanced level? Sometimes this is indicated by such words as "Junior" or "Senior" in the class title. Other jurisdictions use Roman numerals to designate the level – Clerk I, Clerk II, for example. The word "Supervisor" sometimes appears in the title. If the level is not indicated by the title, check the description of duties. Will you be working under very close supervision, or will you have responsibility for independent decisions in this work?

4) Choose appropriate study materials

Now that you know the subjects to be examined and the relative amount of each subject to be covered, you can choose suitable study materials. For beginning level jobs, or even advanced ones, if you have a pronounced weakness in some aspect of your training, read a modern, standard textbook in that field. Be sure it is up to date and has general coverage. Such books are normally available at your library, and the librarian will be glad to help you locate one. For entry-level positions, questions of appropriate difficulty are chosen – neither highly advanced questions, nor those too simple. Such questions require careful thought but not advanced training.

If the position for which you are applying is technical or advanced, you will read more advanced, specialized material. If you are already familiar with the basic principles of your field, elementary textbooks would waste your time. Concentrate on advanced textbooks and technical periodicals. Think through the concepts and review difficult problems in your field.

These are all general sources. You can get more ideas on your own initiative, following these leads. For example, training manuals and publications of the government agency which employs workers in your field can be useful, particularly for technical and professional positions. A letter or visit to the government department involved may result in more specific study suggestions, and certainly will provide you with a more definite idea of the exact nature of the position you are seeking.

III. KINDS OF TESTS

Tests are used for purposes other than measuring knowledge and ability to perform specified duties. For some positions, it is equally important to test ability to make adjustments to new situations or to profit from training. In others, basic mental abilities not dependent on information are essential. Questions which test these things may not appear as pertinent to the duties of the position as those which test for knowledge and information. Yet they are often highly important parts of a fair examination. For very general questions, it is almost impossible to help you direct your study efforts. What we can do is to point out some of the more common of these general abilities needed in public service positions and describe some typical questions.

1) General information

Broad, general information has been found useful for predicting job success in some kinds of work. This is tested in a variety of ways, from vocabulary lists to questions about current events. Basic background in some field of work, such as sociology or economics, may be sampled in a group of questions. Often these are principles which have become familiar to most persons through exposure rather than through formal training. It is difficult to advise you how to study for these questions; being alert to the world around you is our best suggestion.

2) Verbal ability

An example of an ability needed in many positions is verbal or language ability. Verbal ability is, in brief, the ability to use and understand words. Vocabulary and grammar tests are typical measures of this ability. Reading comprehension or paragraph interpretation questions are common in many kinds of civil service tests. You are given a paragraph of written material and asked to find its central meaning.

3) Numerical ability

Number skills can be tested by the familiar arithmetic problem, by checking paired lists of numbers to see which are alike and which are different, or by interpreting charts and graphs. In the latter test, a graph may be printed in the test booklet which you are asked to use as the basis for answering questions.

4) Observation

A popular test for law-enforcement positions is the observation test. A picture is shown to you for several minutes, then taken away. Questions about the picture test your ability to observe both details and larger elements.

5) Following directions

In many positions in the public service, the employee must be able to carry out written instructions dependably and accurately. You may be given a chart with several columns, each column listing a variety of information. The questions require you to carry out directions involving the information given in the chart.

6) Skills and aptitudes

Performance tests effectively measure some manual skills and aptitudes. When the skill is one in which you are trained, such as typing or shorthand, you can practice. These tests are often very much like those given in business school or high school courses. For many of the other skills and aptitudes, however, no short-time preparation can be made. Skills and abilities natural to you or that you have developed throughout your lifetime are being tested.

Many of the general questions just described provide all the data needed to answer the questions and ask you to use your reasoning ability to find the answers. Your best preparation for these tests, as well as for tests of facts and ideas, is to be at your physical and mental best. You, no doubt, have your own methods of getting into an exam-taking mood and keeping "in shape." The next section lists some ideas on this subject.

IV. KINDS OF QUESTIONS

Only rarely is the "essay" question, which you answer in narrative form, used in civil service tests. Civil service tests are usually of the short-answer type. Full instructions for answering these questions will be given to you at the examination. But in case this is your first experience with short-answer questions and separate answer sheets, here is what you need to know:

1) Multiple-choice Questions

Most popular of the short-answer questions is the "multiple choice" or "best answer" question. It can be used, for example, to test for factual knowledge, ability to solve problems or judgment in meeting situations found at work.

A multiple-choice question is normally one of three types—
- It can begin with an incomplete statement followed by several possible endings. You are to find the one ending which *best* completes the statement, although some of the others may not be entirely wrong.
- It can also be a complete statement in the form of a question which is answered by choosing one of the statements listed.

- It can be in the form of a problem – again you select the best answer.

Here is an example of a multiple-choice question with a discussion which should give you some clues as to the method for choosing the right answer:

When an employee has a complaint about his assignment, the action which will *best* help him overcome his difficulty is to
    A. discuss his difficulty with his coworkers
    B. take the problem to the head of the organization
    C. take the problem to the person who gave him the assignment
    D. say nothing to anyone about his complaint

In answering this question, you should study each of the choices to find which is best. Consider choice "A" – Certainly an employee may discuss his complaint with fellow employees, but no change or improvement can result, and the complaint remains unresolved. Choice "B" is a poor choice since the head of the organization probably does not know what assignment you have been given, and taking your problem to him is known as "going over the head" of the supervisor. The supervisor, or person who made the assignment, is the person who can clarify it or correct any injustice. Choice "C" is, therefore, correct. To say nothing, as in choice "D," is unwise. Supervisors have and interest in knowing the problems employees are facing, and the employee is seeking a solution to his problem.

2) True/False Questions

The "true/false" or "right/wrong" form of question is sometimes used. Here a complete statement is given. Your job is to decide whether the statement is right or wrong.

SAMPLE: A roaming cell-phone call to a nearby city costs less than a non-roaming call to a distant city.

This statement is wrong, or false, since roaming calls are more expensive.
This is not a complete list of all possible question forms, although most of the others are variations of these common types. You will always get complete directions for answering questions. Be sure you understand *how* to mark your answers – ask questions until you do.

V. RECORDING YOUR ANSWERS

Computer terminals are used more and more today for many different kinds of exams.
For an examination with very few applicants, you may be told to record your answers in the test booklet itself. Separate answer sheets are much more common. If this separate answer sheet is to be scored by machine – and this is often the case – it is highly important that you mark your answers correctly in order to get credit.
An electronic scoring machine is often used in civil service offices because of the speed with which papers can be scored. Machine-scored answer sheets must be marked with a pencil, which will be given to you. This pencil has a high graphite content which responds to the electronic scoring machine. As a matter of fact, stray dots may register as answers, so do not let your pencil rest on the answer sheet while you are pondering the correct answer. Also, if your pencil lead breaks or is otherwise defective, ask for another.

Since the answer sheet will be dropped in a slot in the scoring machine, be careful not to bend the corners or get the paper crumpled.

The answer sheet normally has five vertical columns of numbers, with 30 numbers to a column. These numbers correspond to the question numbers in your test booklet. After each number, going across the page are four or five pairs of dotted lines. These short dotted lines have small letters or numbers above them. The first two pairs may also have a "T" or "F" above the letters. This indicates that the first two pairs only are to be used if the questions are of the true-false type. If the questions are multiple choice, disregard the "T" and "F" and pay attention only to the small letters or numbers.

Answer your questions in the manner of the sample that follows:

32. The largest city in the United States is
    A. Washington, D.C.
    B. New York City
    C. Chicago
    D. Detroit
    E. San Francisco

1) Choose the answer you think is best. (New York City is the largest, so "B" is correct.)
2) Find the row of dotted lines numbered the same as the question you are answering. (Find row number 32)
3) Find the pair of dotted lines corresponding to the answer. (Find the pair of lines under the mark "B.")
4) Make a solid black mark between the dotted lines.

VI. BEFORE THE TEST

Common sense will help you find procedures to follow to get ready for an examination. Too many of us, however, overlook these sensible measures. Indeed, nervousness and fatigue have been found to be the most serious reasons why applicants fail to do their best on civil service tests. Here is a list of reminders:

- Begin your preparation early – Don't wait until the last minute to go scurrying around for books and materials or to find out what the position is all about.
- Prepare continuously – An hour a night for a week is better than an all-night cram session. This has been definitely established. What is more, a night a week for a month will return better dividends than crowding your study into a shorter period of time.
- Locate the place of the exam – You have been sent a notice telling you when and where to report for the examination. If the location is in a different town or otherwise unfamiliar to you, it would be well to inquire the best route and learn something about the building.
- Relax the night before the test – Allow your mind to rest. Do not study at all that night. Plan some mild recreation or diversion; then go to bed early and get a good night's sleep.
- Get up early enough to make a leisurely trip to the place for the test – This way unforeseen events, traffic snarls, unfamiliar buildings, etc. will not upset you.
- Dress comfortably – A written test is not a fashion show. You will be known by number and not by name, so wear something comfortable.

- Leave excess paraphernalia at home – Shopping bags and odd bundles will get in your way. You need bring only the items mentioned in the official notice you received; usually everything you need is provided. Do not bring reference books to the exam. They will only confuse those last minutes and be taken away from you when in the test room.
- Arrive somewhat ahead of time – If because of transportation schedules you must get there very early, bring a newspaper or magazine to take your mind off yourself while waiting.
- Locate the examination room – When you have found the proper room, you will be directed to the seat or part of the room where you will sit. Sometimes you are given a sheet of instructions to read while you are waiting. Do not fill out any forms until you are told to do so; just read them and be prepared.
- Relax and prepare to listen to the instructions
- If you have any physical problem that may keep you from doing your best, be sure to tell the test administrator. If you are sick or in poor health, you really cannot do your best on the exam. You can come back and take the test some other time.

VII. AT THE TEST

The day of the test is here and you have the test booklet in your hand. The temptation to get going is very strong. Caution! There is more to success than knowing the right answers. You must know how to identify your papers and understand variations in the type of short-answer question used in this particular examination. Follow these suggestions for maximum results from your efforts:

1) Cooperate with the monitor
The test administrator has a duty to create a situation in which you can be as much at ease as possible. He will give instructions, tell you when to begin, check to see that you are marking your answer sheet correctly, and so on. He is not there to guard you, although he will see that your competitors do not take unfair advantage. He wants to help you do your best.

2) Listen to all instructions
Don't jump the gun! Wait until you understand all directions. In most civil service tests you get more time than you need to answer the questions. So don't be in a hurry. Read each word of instructions until you clearly understand the meaning. Study the examples, listen to all announcements and follow directions. Ask questions if you do not understand what to do.

3) Identify your papers
Civil service exams are usually identified by number only. You will be assigned a number; you must not put your name on your test papers. Be sure to copy your number correctly. Since more than one exam may be given, copy your exact examination title.

4) Plan your time
Unless you are told that a test is a "speed" or "rate of work" test, speed itself is usually not important. Time enough to answer all the questions will be provided, but this does not mean that you have all day. An overall time limit has been set. Divide the total time (in minutes) by the number of questions to determine the approximate time you have for each question.

5) Do not linger over difficult questions

If you come across a difficult question, mark it with a paper clip (useful to have along) and come back to it when you have been through the booklet. One caution if you do this – be sure to skip a number on your answer sheet as well. Check often to be sure that you have not lost your place and that you are marking in the row numbered the same as the question you are answering.

6) Read the questions

Be sure you know what the question asks! Many capable people are unsuccessful because they failed to *read* the questions correctly.

7) Answer all questions

Unless you have been instructed that a penalty will be deducted for incorrect answers, it is better to guess than to omit a question.

8) Speed tests

It is often better NOT to guess on speed tests. It has been found that on timed tests people are tempted to spend the last few seconds before time is called in marking answers at random – without even reading them – in the hope of picking up a few extra points. To discourage this practice, the instructions may warn you that your score will be "corrected" for guessing. That is, a penalty will be applied. The incorrect answers will be deducted from the correct ones, or some other penalty formula will be used.

9) Review your answers

If you finish before time is called, go back to the questions you guessed or omitted to give them further thought. Review other answers if you have time.

10) Return your test materials

If you are ready to leave before others have finished or time is called, take ALL your materials to the monitor and leave quietly. Never take any test material with you. The monitor can discover whose papers are not complete, and taking a test booklet may be grounds for disqualification.

VIII. EXAMINATION TECHNIQUES

1) Read the general instructions carefully. These are usually printed on the first page of the exam booklet. As a rule, these instructions refer to the timing of the examination; the fact that you should not start work until the signal and must stop work at a signal, etc. If there are any *special* instructions, such as a choice of questions to be answered, make sure that you note this instruction carefully.

2) When you are ready to start work on the examination, that is as soon as the signal has been given, read the instructions to each question booklet, underline any key words or phrases, such as *least, best, outline, describe* and the like. In this way you will tend to answer as requested rather than discover on reviewing your paper that you *listed without describing*, that you selected the *worst* choice rather than the *best* choice, etc.

3) If the examination is of the objective or multiple-choice type – that is, each question will also give a series of possible answers: A, B, C or D, and you are called upon to select the best answer and write the letter next to that answer on your answer paper – it is advisable to start answering each question in turn. There may be anywhere from 50 to 100 such questions in the three or four hours allotted and you can see how much time would be taken if you read through all the questions before beginning to answer any. Furthermore, if you come across a question or group of questions which you know would be difficult to answer, it would undoubtedly affect your handling of all the other questions.

4) If the examination is of the essay type and contains but a few questions, it is a moot point as to whether you should read all the questions before starting to answer any one. Of course, if you are given a choice – say five out of seven and the like – then it is essential to read all the questions so you can eliminate the two that are most difficult. If, however, you are asked to answer all the questions, there may be danger in trying to answer the easiest one first because you may find that you will spend too much time on it. The best technique is to answer the first question, then proceed to the second, etc.

5) Time your answers. Before the exam begins, write down the time it started, then add the time allowed for the examination and write down the time it must be completed, then divide the time available somewhat as follows:
    - If 3-1/2 hours are allowed, that would be 210 minutes. If you have 80 objective-type questions, that would be an average of 2-1/2 minutes per question. Allow yourself no more than 2 minutes per question, or a total of 160 minutes, which will permit about 50 minutes to review.
    - If for the time allotment of 210 minutes there are 7 essay questions to answer, that would average about 30 minutes a question. Give yourself only 25 minutes per question so that you have about 35 minutes to review.

6) The most important instruction is to *read each question* and make sure you know what is wanted. The second most important instruction is to *time yourself properly* so that you answer every question. The third most important instruction is to *answer every question*. Guess if you have to but include something for each question. Remember that you will receive no credit for a blank and will probably receive some credit if you write something in answer to an essay question. If you guess a letter – say "B" for a multiple-choice question – you may have guessed right. If you leave a blank as an answer to a multiple-choice question, the examiners may respect your feelings but it will not add a point to your score. Some exams may penalize you for wrong answers, so in such cases *only*, you may not want to guess unless you have some basis for your answer.

7) Suggestions
    a. Objective-type questions
        1. Examine the question booklet for proper sequence of pages and questions
        2. Read all instructions carefully
        3. Skip any question which seems too difficult; return to it after all other questions have been answered
        4. Apportion your time properly; do not spend too much time on any single question or group of questions

5. Note and underline key words – *all, most, fewest, least, best, worst, same, opposite,* etc.
6. Pay particular attention to negatives
7. Note unusual option, e.g., unduly long, short, complex, different or similar in content to the body of the question
8. Observe the use of "hedging" words – *probably, may, most likely,* etc.
9. Make sure that your answer is put next to the same number as the question
10. Do not second-guess unless you have good reason to believe the second answer is definitely more correct
11. Cross out original answer if you decide another answer is more accurate; do not erase until you are ready to hand your paper in
12. Answer all questions; guess unless instructed otherwise
13. Leave time for review

b. Essay questions
1. Read each question carefully
2. Determine exactly what is wanted. Underline key words or phrases.
3. Decide on outline or paragraph answer
4. Include many different points and elements unless asked to develop any one or two points or elements
5. Show impartiality by giving pros and cons unless directed to select one side only
6. Make and write down any assumptions you find necessary to answer the questions
7. Watch your English, grammar, punctuation and choice of words
8. Time your answers; don't crowd material

8) Answering the essay question

Most essay questions can be answered by framing the specific response around several key words or ideas. Here are a few such key words or ideas:

M's: manpower, materials, methods, money, management
P's: purpose, program, policy, plan, procedure, practice, problems, pitfalls, personnel, public relations

a. Six basic steps in handling problems:
1. Preliminary plan and background development
2. Collect information, data and facts
3. Analyze and interpret information, data and facts
4. Analyze and develop solutions as well as make recommendations
5. Prepare report and sell recommendations
6. Install recommendations and follow up effectiveness

b. Pitfalls to avoid
1. *Taking things for granted* – A statement of the situation does not necessarily imply that each of the elements is necessarily true; for example, a complaint may be invalid and biased so that all that can be taken for granted is that a complaint has been registered

2. *Considering only one side of a situation* – Wherever possible, indicate several alternatives and then point out the reasons you selected the best one
3. *Failing to indicate follow up* – Whenever your answer indicates action on your part, make certain that you will take proper follow-up action to see how successful your recommendations, procedures or actions turn out to be
4. *Taking too long in answering any single question* – Remember to time your answers properly

IX. AFTER THE TEST

Scoring procedures differ in detail among civil service jurisdictions although the general principles are the same. Whether the papers are hand-scored or graded by machine we have described, they are nearly always graded by number. That is, the person who marks the paper knows only the number – never the name – of the applicant. Not until all the papers have been graded will they be matched with names. If other tests, such as training and experience or oral interview ratings have been given, scores will be combined. Different parts of the examination usually have different weights. For example, the written test might count 60 percent of the final grade, and a rating of training and experience 40 percent. In many jurisdictions, veterans will have a certain number of points added to their grades.

After the final grade has been determined, the names are placed in grade order and an eligible list is established. There are various methods for resolving ties between those who get the same final grade – probably the most common is to place first the name of the person whose application was received first. Job offers are made from the eligible list in the order the names appear on it. You will be notified of your grade and your rank as soon as all these computations have been made. This will be done as rapidly as possible.

People who are found to meet the requirements in the announcement are called "eligibles." Their names are put on a list of eligible candidates. An eligible's chances of getting a job depend on how high he stands on this list and how fast agencies are filling jobs from the list.

When a job is to be filled from a list of eligibles, the agency asks for the names of people on the list of eligibles for that job. When the civil service commission receives this request, it sends to the agency the names of the three people highest on this list. Or, if the job to be filled has specialized requirements, the office sends the agency the names of the top three persons who meet these requirements from the general list.

The appointing officer makes a choice from among the three people whose names were sent to him. If the selected person accepts the appointment, the names of the others are put back on the list to be considered for future openings.

That is the rule in hiring from all kinds of eligible lists, whether they are for typist, carpenter, chemist, or something else. For every vacancy, the appointing officer has his choice of any one of the top three eligibles on the list. This explains why the person whose name is on top of the list sometimes does not get an appointment when some of the persons lower on the list do. If the appointing officer chooses the second or third eligible, the No. 1 eligible does not get a job at once, but stays on the list until he is appointed or the list is terminated.

X. HOW TO PASS THE INTERVIEW TEST

The examination for which you applied requires an oral interview test. You have already taken the written test and you are now being called for the interview test – the final part of the formal examination.

You may think that it is not possible to prepare for an interview test and that there are no procedures to follow during an interview. Our purpose is to point out some things you can do in advance that will help you and some good rules to follow and pitfalls to avoid while you are being interviewed.

What is an interview supposed to test?

The written examination is designed to test the technical knowledge and competence of the candidate; the oral is designed to evaluate intangible qualities, not readily measured otherwise, and to establish a list showing the relative fitness of each candidate – as measured against his competitors – for the position sought. Scoring is not on the basis of "right" and "wrong," but on a sliding scale of values ranging from "not passable" to "outstanding." As a matter of fact, it is possible to achieve a relatively low score without a single "incorrect" answer because of evident weakness in the qualities being measured.

Occasionally, an examination may consist entirely of an oral test – either an individual or a group oral. In such cases, information is sought concerning the technical knowledges and abilities of the candidate, since there has been no written examination for this purpose. More commonly, however, an oral test is used to supplement a written examination.

Who conducts interviews?

The composition of oral boards varies among different jurisdictions. In nearly all, a representative of the personnel department serves as chairman. One of the members of the board may be a representative of the department in which the candidate would work. In some cases, "outside experts" are used, and, frequently, a businessman or some other representative of the general public is asked to serve. Labor and management or other special groups may be represented. The aim is to secure the services of experts in the appropriate field.

However the board is composed, it is a good idea (and not at all improper or unethical) to ascertain in advance of the interview who the members are and what groups they represent. When you are introduced to them, you will have some idea of their backgrounds and interests, and at least you will not stutter and stammer over their names.

What should be done before the interview?

While knowledge about the board members is useful and takes some of the surprise element out of the interview, there is other preparation which is more substantive. It *is* possible to prepare for an oral interview – in several ways:

1) Keep a copy of your application and review it carefully before the interview

This may be the only document before the oral board, and the starting point of the interview. Know what education and experience you have listed there, and the sequence and dates of all of it. Sometimes the board will ask you to review the highlights of your experience for them; you should not have to hem and haw doing it.

2) Study the class specification and the examination announcement

Usually, the oral board has one or both of these to guide them. The qualities, characteristics or knowledges required by the position sought are stated in these documents. They offer valuable clues as to the nature of the oral interview. For example, if the job involves supervisory responsibilities, the announcement will usually indicate that knowledge of modern supervisory methods and the qualifications of the candidate as a supervisor will be tested. If so, you can expect such questions, frequently in the form of a hypothetical situation which you are expected to solve. NEVER go into an oral without knowledge of the duties and responsibilities of the job you seek.

3) Think through each qualification required

Try to visualize the kind of questions you would ask if you were a board member. How well could you answer them? Try especially to appraise your own knowledge and background in each area, *measured against the job sought*, and identify any areas in which you are weak. Be critical and realistic – do not flatter yourself.

4) Do some general reading in areas in which you feel you may be weak

For example, if the job involves supervision and your past experience has NOT, some general reading in supervisory methods and practices, particularly in the field of human relations, might be useful. Do NOT study agency procedures or detailed manuals. The oral board will be testing your understanding and capacity, not your memory.

5) Get a good night's sleep and watch your general health and mental attitude

You will want a clear head at the interview. Take care of a cold or any other minor ailment, and of course, no hangovers.

What should be done on the day of the interview?

Now comes the day of the interview itself. Give yourself plenty of time to get there. Plan to arrive somewhat ahead of the scheduled time, particularly if your appointment is in the fore part of the day. If a previous candidate fails to appear, the board might be ready for you a bit early. By early afternoon an oral board is almost invariably behind schedule if there are many candidates, and you may have to wait. Take along a book or magazine to read, or your application to review, but leave any extraneous material in the waiting room when you go in for your interview. In any event, relax and compose yourself.

The matter of dress is important. The board is forming impressions about you – from your experience, your manners, your attitude, and your appearance. Give your personal appearance careful attention. Dress your best, but not your flashiest. Choose conservative, appropriate clothing, and be sure it is immaculate. This is a business interview, and your appearance should indicate that you regard it as such. Besides, being well groomed and properly dressed will help boost your confidence.

Sooner or later, someone will call your name and escort you into the interview room. *This is it.* From here on you are on your own. It is too late for any more preparation. But remember, you asked for this opportunity to prove your fitness, and you are here because your request was granted.

What happens when you go in?

The usual sequence of events will be as follows: The clerk (who is often the board stenographer) will introduce you to the chairman of the oral board, who will introduce you to the other members of the board. Acknowledge the introductions before you sit down. Do not be surprised if you find a microphone facing you or a stenotypist sitting by. Oral interviews are usually recorded in the event of an appeal or other review.

Usually the chairman of the board will open the interview by reviewing the highlights of your education and work experience from your application – primarily for the benefit of the other members of the board, as well as to get the material into the record. Do not interrupt or comment unless there is an error or significant misinterpretation; if that is the case, do not hesitate. But do not quibble about insignificant matters. Also, he will usually ask you some question about your education, experience or your present job – partly to get you to start talking and to establish the interviewing "rapport." He may start the actual questioning, or turn it over to one of the other members. Frequently, each member undertakes the questioning on a particular area, one in which he is perhaps most competent, so you can expect each member to participate in the examination. Because time is limited, you may also expect some rather abrupt switches in the direction the questioning takes, so do not be upset by it. Normally, a board member will not pursue a single line of questioning unless he discovers a particular strength or weakness.

After each member has participated, the chairman will usually ask whether any member has any further questions, then will ask you if you have anything you wish to add. Unless you are expecting this question, it may floor you. Worse, it may start you off on an extended, extemporaneous speech. The board is not usually seeking more information. The question is principally to offer you a last opportunity to present further qualifications or to indicate that you have nothing to add. So, if you feel that a significant qualification or characteristic has been overlooked, it is proper to point it out in a sentence or so. Do not compliment the board on the thoroughness of their examination – they have been sketchy, and you know it. If you wish, merely say, "No thank you, I have nothing further to add." This is a point where you can "talk yourself out" of a good impression or fail to present an important bit of information. Remember, *you close the interview yourself.*

The chairman will then say, "That is all, Mr. _____, thank you." Do not be startled; the interview is over, and quicker than you think. Thank him, gather your belongings and take your leave. Save your sigh of relief for the other side of the door.

How to put your best foot forward
Throughout this entire process, you may feel that the board individually and collectively is trying to pierce your defenses, seek out your hidden weaknesses and embarrass and confuse you. Actually, this is not true. They are obliged to make an appraisal of your qualifications for the job you are seeking, and they want to see you in your best light. Remember, they must interview all candidates and a non-cooperative candidate may become a failure in spite of their best efforts to bring out his qualifications. Here are 15 suggestions that will help you:

1) Be natural – Keep your attitude confident, not cocky
If you are not confident that you can do the job, do not expect the board to be. Do not apologize for your weaknesses, try to bring out your strong points. The board is interested in a positive, not negative, presentation. Cockiness will antagonize any board member and make him wonder if you are covering up a weakness by a false show of strength.

2) Get comfortable, but don't lounge or sprawl
Sit erectly but not stiffly. A careless posture may lead the board to conclude that you are careless in other things, or at least that you are not impressed by the importance of the occasion. Either conclusion is natural, even if incorrect. Do not fuss with your clothing, a pencil or an ashtray. Your hands may occasionally be useful to emphasize a point; do not let them become a point of distraction.

3) Do not wisecrack or make small talk
This is a serious situation, and your attitude should show that you consider it as such. Further, the time of the board is limited – they do not want to waste it, and neither should you.

4) Do not exaggerate your experience or abilities

In the first place, from information in the application or other interviews and sources, the board may know more about you than you think. Secondly, you probably will not get away with it. An experienced board is rather adept at spotting such a situation, so do not take the chance.

5) If you know a board member, do not make a point of it, yet do not hide it

Certainly you are not fooling him, and probably not the other members of the board. Do not try to take advantage of your acquaintanceship – it will probably do you little good.

6) Do not dominate the interview

Let the board do that. They will give you the clues – do not assume that you have to do all the talking. Realize that the board has a number of questions to ask you, and do not try to take up all the interview time by showing off your extensive knowledge of the answer to the first one.

7) Be attentive

You only have 20 minutes or so, and you should keep your attention at its sharpest throughout. When a member is addressing a problem or question to you, give him your undivided attention. Address your reply principally to him, but do not exclude the other board members.

8) Do not interrupt

A board member may be stating a problem for you to analyze. He will ask you a question when the time comes. Let him state the problem, and wait for the question.

9) Make sure you understand the question

Do not try to answer until you are sure what the question is. If it is not clear, restate it in your own words or ask the board member to clarify it for you. However, do not haggle about minor elements.

10) Reply promptly but not hastily

A common entry on oral board rating sheets is "candidate responded readily," or "candidate hesitated in replies." Respond as promptly and quickly as you can, but do not jump to a hasty, ill-considered answer.

11) Do not be peremptory in your answers

A brief answer is proper – but do not fire your answer back. That is a losing game from your point of view. The board member can probably ask questions much faster than you can answer them.

12) Do not try to create the answer you think the board member wants

He is interested in what kind of mind you have and how it works – not in playing games. Furthermore, he can usually spot this practice and will actually grade you down on it.

13) Do not switch sides in your reply merely to agree with a board member

Frequently, a member will take a contrary position merely to draw you out and to see if you are willing and able to defend your point of view. Do not start a debate, yet do not surrender a good position. If a position is worth taking, it is worth defending.

14) Do not be afraid to admit an error in judgment if you are shown to be wrong

The board knows that you are forced to reply without any opportunity for careful consideration. Your answer may be demonstrably wrong. If so, admit it and get on with the interview.

15) Do not dwell at length on your present job

The opening question may relate to your present assignment. Answer the question but do not go into an extended discussion. You are being examined for a *new* job, not your present one. As a matter of fact, try to phrase ALL your answers in terms of the job for which you are being examined.

Basis of Rating

Probably you will forget most of these "do's" and "don'ts" when you walk into the oral interview room. Even remembering them all will not ensure you a passing grade. Perhaps you did not have the qualifications in the first place. But remembering them will help you to put your best foot forward, without treading on the toes of the board members.

Rumor and popular opinion to the contrary notwithstanding, an oral board wants you to make the best appearance possible. They know you are under pressure – but they also want to see how you respond to it as a guide to what your reaction would be under the pressures of the job you seek. They will be influenced by the degree of poise you display, the personal traits you show and the manner in which you respond.

ABOUT THIS BOOK

This book contains tests divided into Examination Sections. Go through each test, answering every question in the margin. We have also attached a sample answer sheet at the back of the book that can be removed and used. At the end of each test look at the answer key and check your answers. On the ones you got wrong, look at the right answer choice and learn. Do not fill in the answers first. Do not memorize the questions and answers, but understand the answer and principles involved. On your test, the questions will likely be different from the samples. Questions are changed and new ones added. If you understand these past questions you should have success with any changes that arise. Tests may consist of several types of questions. We have additional books on each subject should more study be advisable or necessary for you. Finally, the more you study, the better prepared you will be. This book is intended to be the last thing you study before you walk into the examination room. Prior study of relevant texts is also recommended. NLC publishes some of these in our Fundamental Series. Knowledge and good sense are important factors in passing your exam. Good luck also helps. So now study this Passbook, absorb the material contained within and take that knowledge into the examination. Then do your best to pass that exam.

EXAMINATION SECTION

EXAMINATION SECTION
TEST 1

DIRECTIONS: Each question or incomplete statement is followed by several suggested answers or completions. Select the one that BEST answers the question or completes the statement. *PRINT THE LETTER OF THE CORRECT ANSWER IN THE SPACE AT THE RIGHT.*

Questions 1-5

DIRECTIONS: Questions 1 through 5 are to be answered on the basis of the extracts from Federal income tax withholding and social security tax tables shown below. These tables indicate the amounts which must be withheld from the employee's salary by his employer for Federal income tax and for social security. They are based on weekly earnings.

INCOME TAX WITHHOLDING TABLE

The wages are		And the number of withholding allowances is					
		5	6	7	8	9	10 or more
At least	But less than	The amount of Income tax to be withheld shall be					
$300	$320	$24.60	$19.00	$13.80	$ 8.60	$ 4.00	$ 0
320	340	28.80	22.80	17.40	12.20	7.00	2.80
340	360	33.00	27.00	21.00	15.80	10.60	5.60
360	380	37.20	31.20	25.20	19.40	14.20	9.00
380	400	41.40	35.40	29.40	23.40	17.80	12.60
400	420	45.60	39.60	33.60	27.60	21.40	16.20
420	440	49.80	43.80	37.80	31.80	25.60	19.80
440	460	54.00	48.00	42.00	36.00	29.80	23.80
460	480	58.20	52.20	46.20	40.20	34.00	38.00
480	500	62.40	56.40	50.40	44.40	38.20	32.20

SOCIAL SECURITY TABLE

WAGES			WAGES		Tax
At least	But less than	Tax to be withheld	At least	But less than	to be withheld
$333.18	$333.52	$19.50	$336.60	$336.94	$19.70
333.52	333.86	19.52	336.94	337.28	19.72
333.86	334.20	19.54	337.28	337.62	19.74
334.20	334.54	19.56	337.62	337.96	19.76
334.54	334.88	19.58	337.96	338.30	19.78
334.88	335.22	19.60	338.30	338.64	19.80
335.22	335.56	19.62	338.64	338.98	19.82
335.56	335.90	19.64	338.98	339.32	19.84
335.90	336.24	19.66	339.32	339.66	19.86
336.24	336.60	19.68	339.66	340.00	19.88

1. If an employee has a weekly wage of $379.50 and claims 6 withholding allowances, the amount of income tax to be withheld is

   A. $27.00   B. $31.20   C. $35.40   D. $37.20

2. An employee had wages of $335.60 for one week.
   With eight withholding allowances claimed, how much income tax will be withheld from his salary?

   A. $8.60   B. $12.20   C. $13.80   D. $17.40

3. How much social security tax will an employee with weekly wages of $335.60 pay?

   A. $19.60   B. $19.62   C. $19.64   D. $19.66

4. Mr. Wise earns $339.80 a week and claims seven withholding allowances.
   What is his take-home pay after income tax and social security tax are deducted?

   A. $300.32   B. $302.52   C. $319.92   D. $322.40

5. If an employee pays $19.74 in social security tax and claims eight withholding allowances, the amount of income tax that should be withheld from his wages is

   A. $8.60   B. $12.20   C. $13.80   D. $15.80

6. A fundamental rule of bookkeeping states that an individual's assets equal his liabilities plus his proprietorship (ASSETS = LIABILITIES + PROPRIETORSHIP).
   Which of the following statements logically follows from this rule?

   A. ASSETS = PROPRIETORSHIP - LIABILITIES
   B. LIABILITIES = ASSETS + PROPRIETORSHIP
   C. PROPRIETORSHIP = ASSETS - LIABILITIES
   D. PROPRIETORSHIP = LIABILITIES + ASSETS

7. Mr. Martin's assets consist of the following:
   Cash on hand: $5,233.74
   Furniture: $4,925.00
   Government Bonds: $5,500.00
   What are his TOTAL assets?

   A. $10,158.74   B. $10,425.00
   C. $10,733.74   D. $15,658.74

8. If Mr. Mitchell has $627.04 in his checking account and then writes three checks for $241.75, $13.24, and $102.97, what will be his new balance?

   A. $257.88   B. $269.08   C. $357.96   D. $369.96

9. An employee's net pay is equal to his total earnings less all deductions.
   If an employee's total earnings in a pay period are $497.05, what is his NET pay if he has the following deductions:
   Federal income tax, $90.32; FICA, $28.74; State tax, $18.79; City tax, $7.25; Pension, $1.88?

   A. $351.17   B. $351.07   C. $350.17   D. $350.07

10. A petty cash fund had an opening balance of $85.75 on December 1. Expenditures of $23.00, $15.65, $5.23, $14.75, and $26.38 were made out of this fund during the first 14 days of the month. Then, on December 17, another $38.50 was added to the fund. If additional expenditures of $17.18, $3.29, and $11.64 were made during the remainder of the month, what was the FINAL balance of the petty cash fund at the end of December?   10._____

    A. $6.93   B. $7.13   C. $46.51   D. $91.40

Questions 11-15.

DIRECTIONS: Questions 11 through 15 are to be answered on the basis of the following instructions.

The chart below is used by the loan division of a city retirement system for the following purposes: (1) to calculate the monthly payment a member must pay on an outstanding loan; (2) to calculate how much a member owes on an outstanding loan after he has made a number of payments.

To calculate the amount a member must pay each month in repaying his loan, look at Column II on the chart. You will notice that each entry in Column II corresponds to a number appearing under the *Months* column; for example, 1.004868 corresponds to 1 month, 0.503654 corresponds to 2 months, etc. To calculate the amount a member must pay each month, use the following procedure: multiply the amount of the loan by the entry in Column II which corresponds to the number of months over which the loan will be paid back. For example, if a loan of $200 is taken out for six months, multiply $200 by 0.169518, the entry in Column II which corresponds to six months.

In order to calculate the balance still owed on an outstanding loan, multiply the monthly payment by the number in Column I which corresponds to the number of monthly payments which remain to be paid on the loan. For example, if a member is supposed to pay $106.00 a month for twelve months, after seven payments, five monthly payments remain. To calculate the balance owed on the loan at this point, multiply the $106.00 monthly payment by 4.927807, the number in Column I that corresponds to five months.

Months	Column I	Column II
1	0.995156	1.004868
2	1.985491	0.503654
3	2.971029	0.336584
4	3.951793	0.253050
5	4.927807	0.202930
6	5.899092	0.169518
7	6.865673	0.145652
8	7.827572	0.127754
9	8.784811	0.113833
10	9.737414	0.102697
11	10.685402	0.093586
12	11.628798	0.085993
13	12.567624	0.079570
14	13.501902	0.074064
15	14.431655	0.069292

11. If Mr. Carson borrows $1,500 for eight months, how much will he have to pay back each month?

    A. $187.16   B. $191.63   C. $208.72   D. $218.65

12. If a member borrows $2,400 for one year, the amount he will have to pay back each month is

    A. $118.78   B. $196.18   C. $202.28   D. $206.38

13. Mr. Elliott borrowed $1,700 for a period of fifteen months.
    Each month he will have to pay back

    A. $117.80   B. $116.96   C. $107.79   D. $101.79

14. Mr. Aylward is paying back a thirteen-month loan at the rate of $173.13 a month. If he has already made six monthly payments, how much does he owe on the outstanding loan?

    A. $1,027.39   B. $1,178.75   C. $1,188.65   D. $1,898.85

15. A loan was taken out for 15 months, and the monthly payment was $104.75. After two monthly payments, how much was still owed on this loan?

    A. $515.79   B. $863.89   C. $1,116.76   D. $1,316.46

16. The ABC Corporation had a gross income of $125,500.00 in 2005. Of this, it paid 60% for overhead.
    If the gross income for 2006 increased by $6,500 and the cost of overhead increased to 61% of gross income, how much more did it pay for overhead in 2006 than in 2005?

    A. $1,320   B. $5,220   C. $7,530   D. $8,052

17. After one year, Mr. Richards paid back a total of $1,695.00 as payment for a $1,500.00 loan. All the money paid over $1,500.00 was simple interest.
    The interest charge was MOST NEARLY

    A. 13%   B. 11%   C. 9%   D. 7%

18. A checking account has a balance of $253.36.
    If deposits of $36.95, $210.23, and $7.34 and withdrawals of $117.35, $23.37, and $15.98 are made, what is the NEW balance of the account?

    A. $155.54   B. $351.18   C. $364.58   D. $664.58

19. In 2005, the W Realty Company spent 27% of its income on rent.
    If it earned $97,254.00 in 2005, the amount it paid for rent was

    A. $26,258.58   B. $26,348.58
    C. $27,248.58   D. $27,358.58

20. Six percent simple annual interest on $2,436.18 is MOST NEARLY

    A. $145.08   B. $145.17   C. $146.08   D. $146.17

21. Assume that the XYZ Company has $10,402.72 cash on hand. If it pays $699.83 of this for rent, the amount of cash on hand would be 21.____

    A. $9,792.89
    C. $9,692.89
    B. $9,702.89
    D. $9,602.89

22. On January 31, Mr. Warren's checking account had a balance of $933.68. If he deposited $36.40 on February 2, $126.00 on February 9, and $90.02 on February 16, and wrote no checks during this period, what was the balance of his account on February 17? 22.____

    A. $680.26   B. $681.26   C. $1,186.10   D. $1,187.00

23. Multiplying a number by .75 is the same as 23.____

    A. *multiplying* it by 2/3
    C. *multiplying* it by 3/4
    B. *dividing* it by 2/3
    D. *dividing* it by 3/4

24. In City Agency A, 2/3 of the employees are enrolled in a retirement system. City Agency B has the same number of employees as Agency A, and 60% of these are enrolled in a retirement system. 24.____
    If Agency A has a total of 660 employees, how many MORE employees does it have enrolled in a retirement system than does Agency B?

    A. 36   B. 44   C. 56   D. 66

25. Net Worth is equal to Assets minus Liabilities. 25.____
    If, at the end of year, a textile company had assets of $98,695.83 and liabilities of $59,238.29, what was its net worth?

    A. $38,478.54
    C. $39,457.54
    B. $38,488.64
    D. $48,557.54

KEY (CORRECT ANSWERS)

1.	B	11.	B
2.	B	12.	D
3.	C	13.	A
4.	B	14.	C
5.	B	15.	D
6.	C	16.	B
7.	D	17.	A
8.	B	18.	B
9.	D	19.	A
10.	B	20.	D

21. B
22. C
23. C
24. B
25. C

TEST 2

DIRECTIONS: Each question or incomplete statement is followed by several suggested answers or completions. Select the one that BEST answers the question or completes the statement. *PRINT THE LETTER OF THE CORRECT ANSWER IN THE SPACE AT THE RIGHT.*

Questions 1-10.

DIRECTIONS: Questions 1 through 10 below present the identification numbers, initials, and last names of employees enrolled in a city retirement system. You are to choose the option (A, B, C, or D) that has the IDENTICAL identification number, initials, and last name as those given in each question.

Sample Question
B145698 JL Jones
- A. B146798 JL Jones
- B. B145698 JL Jonas
- C. P145698 JL Jones
- D. B145698 JL Jones

The correct answer is D. Only Option D shows the identification number, initials, and last name exactly as they are in the sample question. Options A, B, and C have errors in the identification number or last name.

1. J297483 PL Robinson
   - A. J294783 PL Robinson
   - B. J297483 PL Robinson
   - C. J297483 Pl Robinson
   - D. J297843 PL Robinson

2. S497662 JG Schwartz
   - A. S497662 JG Schwarz
   - B. S497762 JG Schwartz
   - C. S497662 JG Schwartz
   - D. S497663 JG Schwartz

3. G696436 LN Alberton
   - A. G696436 LM Alberton
   - B. G696436 LN Albertson
   - C. G696346 LN Albertson
   - D. G696436 LN Alberton

4. R774923 AD Aldrich
   - A. R774923 AD Aldrich
   - B. R744923 AD Aldrich
   - C. R774932 AP Aldrich
   - D. R774932 AD Allrich

5. N239638 RP Hrynyk
   - A. N236938 PR Hrynyk
   - B. N236938 RP Hrynyk
   - C. N239638 PR Hrynyk
   - D. N239638 RP Hrynyk

6. R156949 LT Carlson
   - A. R156949 LT Carlton
   - B. R156494 LT Carlson
   - C. R159649 LT Carlton
   - D. R156949 LT Carlson

7. T524697 MN Orenstein
   - A. T524697 MN Orenstein
   - B. T524967 MN Orinstein
   - C. T524697 NM Ornstein
   - D. T524967 NM Orenstein

1.___

2.___

3.___

4.___

5.___

6.___

7.___

8. L346239 JD Remsen

   A. L346239 JD Remson
   B. L364239 JD Remsen
   C. L346329 JD Remsen
   D. L346239 JD Remsen

8.____

9. P966438 SB Rieperson

   A. P996438 SB Reiperson
   B. P966438 SB Reiperson
   C. R996438 SB Rieperson
   D. P966438 SB Rieperson

9.____

10. D749382 CD Thompson

    A. P749382 CD Thompson
    B. D749832 CD Thomsonn
    C. D749382 CD Thompson
    D. D749823 CD Thomspon

10.____

Questions 11-20.

DIRECTIONS: Assume that each of the capital letters in the table below represents the name of an employee enrolled in the city's employees' personnel system. The number directly beneath the letter represents the agency for which the employee works, and the small letter directly beneath represents the code for the employee's account.

Name of Employee	L	O	T	Q	A	M	R	N	C
Agency	3	4	5	9	8	7	2	1	6
Account Code	r	f	b	i	d	t	g	e	n

In each of the following Questions 11 through 20, the agency code numbers and the account code letters in Columns 2 and 3 should correspond to the capital letters in Column 1 and should be in the same consecutive order. For each question, look at each column carefully and mark your answer as follows:

If there are one or more errors in Column 2 *only,* mark your answer A.
If there are one or more errors in Column 3 *only,* mark your answer B.
If there are one or more errors in Column 2 and one or more errors in Column 3, mark your answer C.
If there are NO errors in either column, mark your answer D.

SAMPLE QUESTION

Column 1   Column 2   Column 3
T Q L M O C   5 8 3 7 4 6   b i r t f n

In Column 2, the second agency code number (corresponding to letter Q) should be 9, not 8. Column 3 is coded correctly to Column 1. Since there is an error only in Column 2, the correct answer is A.

	COLUMN 1	COLUMN 2	COLUMN 3	
11.	Q L N R C A	9 3 1 2 6 8	i r e g n d	11.__
12.	N R M O T C	1 2 7 5 4 6	e g f t b n	12.__
13.	R C T A L M	2 6 5 8 3 7	g n d b r t	13.__
14.	T A M L O N	5 7 8 3 4 1	b d t r f e	14.__
15.	A N T O R M	8 1 5 4 2 7	d e b i g t	15.__
16.	M R A L O N	7 2 8 3 4 1	t g d r f e	16.__
17.	C T N Q R O	6 5 7 9 2 4	n d e i g f	17.__
18.	Q M R O T A	9 7 2 4 5 8	i t g f b d	18.__
19.	R Q M C O L	2 9 7 4 6 3	g i t n f r	19.__
20.	N O M R T Q	1 4 7 2 5 9	e f t g b i	20.__

Questions 21-25.

DIRECTIONS: Questions 21 through 25 are to be answered SOLELY on the basis of the following passage.

The city may issue its own bonds or it may purchase bonds as an investment. Bonds may be issued in various denominations, and the face value of the bond is its par value. Before purchasing a bond, the investor desires to know the rate of income that the investment will yield. In computing the yield on a bond, it is assumed that the investor will keep the bond until the date of maturity, except for callable bonds which are not considered in this passage. To compute exact yield is a complicated mathematical problem, and scientifically prepared tables are generally used to avoid such computation. However, the approximate yield can be computed much more easily. In computing approximate yield, the accrued interest on the date of purchase should be ignored because the buyer who pays accrued interest to the seller receives it again at the next interest date. Bonds bought at a premium (which cost more) yield a lower rate of income than the same bonds bought at par (face value), and bonds bought at a discount (which cost less) yield a higher rate of income than the same bonds bought at par.

21. An investor bought a $10,000 city bond paying 6% interest. Which of the following purchase prices would indicate that the bond was bought at a premium?   21.__

    A. $9,000   B. $9,400   C. $10,000   D. $10,600

22. During 2006, a particular $10,000 bond paying 7 1/2% sold at fluctuating prices. Which of the following prices would indicate that the bond was bought at a discount?   22.__

    A. $9,800   B. $10,000   C. $10,200   D. $10,750

4 (#2)

23. A certain group of bonds was sold in denominations of $5,000, $10,000, $20,000, and $50,000.
In the following list of four purchase prices, which one is MOST likely to represent a bond sold at par value?

    A. $10,500   B. $20,000   C. $22,000   D. $49,000

23.____

24. When computing the approximate yield on a bond, it is DESIRABLE to

    A. assume the bond was purchased at par
    B. consult scientifically prepared tables
    C. ignore accrued interest on the date of purchase
    D. wait until the bond reaches maturity

24.____

25. Which of the following is MOST likely to be an exception to the information provided in the above passage?
Bonds

    A. purchased at a premium   B. sold at par
    C. sold before maturity   D. which are callable

25.____

KEY (CORRECT ANSWERS)

1.	B	11.	D
2.	C	12.	C
3.	D	13.	B
4.	A	14.	A
5.	D	15.	B
6.	D	16.	D
7.	A	17.	C
8.	D	18.	D
9.	D	19.	A
10.	C	20.	D

21. D
22. A
23. B
24. C
25. D

TEST 3

DIRECTIONS: Each question or incomplete statement is followed by several suggested answers or completions. Select the one that BEST answers the question or completes the statement. *PRINT THE LETTER OF THE CORRECT ANSWER IN THE SPACE AT THE RIGHT.*

Questions 1-6.

DIRECTIONS: Questions 1 through 6 consist of computations of addition, subtraction, multiplication, and division. For each question, do the computation indicated, and choose the correct answer from the four choices given.

1. ADD: 8936
   7821
   8953
   4297
   9785
   6579

   A. 45371   B. 45381   C. 46371   D. 46381

   1.___

2. SUBTRACT: 95,432
   67,596

   A. 27,836   B. 27,846   C. 27,936   D. 27,946

   2.___

3. MULTIPLY: 987
   867

   A. 854609   B. 854729   C. 855709   D. 855729

   3.___

4. DIVIDE: 59)321439.0

   A. 5438.1   B. 5447.1   C. 5448.1   D. 5457.1

   4.___

5. DIVIDE: .057)721

   A. 12,648.0   B. 12,648.1   C. 12,649.0   D. 12,649.1

   5.___

6. ADD: 1/2 + 5/7

   A. 1 3/14   B. 1 2/7   C. 1 5/14   D. 1 3/7

   6.___

7. If the total number of employees in one city agency increased from 1,927 to 2,006 during a certain year, the percentage increase in the number of employees for that year is MOST NEARLY

   A. 4%   B. 5%   C. 6%   D. 7%

   7.___

8. During a single fiscal year, which totaled 248 workdays, one account clerk verified 1,488 purchase vouchers. Assuming a normal work week of five days, what is the average number of vouchers verified by the account clerk in a one-week period during this fiscal year?

   A. 25 B. 30 C. 35 D. 40

9. If the city department of purchase bought 190 computers for $793.50 each and 208 computers for $839.90 each, the TOTAL price paid for these computers is

   A. $315,813.00 B. $325,464.20
   C. $334,278.20 D. $335.863.00

Questions 10-14.

DIRECTIONS: Questions 10 through 14 are to be answered SOLELY on the basis of the information given in the following paragraph.

Since discounts are in common use in the commercial world and apply to purchases made by government agencies as well as business firms, it is essential that individuals in both public and private employment who prepare bills, check invoices, prepare payment vouchers, or write checks to pay bills have an understanding of the terms used. These include cash or time discount, trade discount, and discount series. A cash or time discount offers a reduction in price to the buyer for the prompt payment of the bill and is usually expressed as a percentage with a time requirement, stated in days, within which the bill must be paid in order to earn the discount. An example would be 3/10, meaning a 3% discount may be applied to the bill if the payment is forwarded to the vendor within ten days. On an invoice, the cash discount terms are usually followed by the net terms, which is the time in days allowed for ordinary payment of the bill. Thus, 3/10, Net 30 means that full payment is expected in thirty days if the cash discount of 3% is not taken for having paid the bill within ten days. When the expression Terms Net Cash is listed on a bill, it means that no deduction for early payment is allowed. A trade discount is normally applied to list prices by a manufacturer to show the actual price to retailers so that they may know their cost and determine markups that will allow them to operate competitively and at a profit. A trade discount is applied by the seller to the list price and is independent of a cash or time discount. Discounts may also be used by manufacturers to adjust prices charged to retailers without changing list prices. This is usually done by series discounting and is expressed as a series of percentages. To compute a series discount, such as 40%, 20%, 10%, first apply the 40% discount to the list price, then apply the 20% discount to the remainder, and finally apply the 10% discount to the second remainder.

10. According to the above passage, trade discounts are

    A. applied by the buyer
    B. independent of cash discounts
    C. restricted to cash sales
    D. used to secure rapid payment of bills

11. According to the above passage, if the sales terms 5/10, Net 60 appear on a bill in the amount of $100 dated December 5, 2006 and the buyer submits his payment on December 15, 2006, his PROPER payment should be

    A. $60 B. $90 C. $95 D. $100

12. According to the above passage, if a manufacturer gives a trade discount of 40% for an item with a list price of $250 and the terms are Net Cash, the price a retail merchant is required to pay for this item is

   A. $250   B. $210   C. $150   D. $100

13. According to the above passage, a series discount of 25%, 20%, 10% applied to a list price of $200 results in an ACTUAL price to the buyer of

   A. $88   B. $90   C. $108   D. $110

14. According to the above passage, if a manufacturer gives a trade discount of 50% and the terms are 6/10, Net 30, the cost to a retail merchant of an item with a list price of $500 and for which he takes the time discount is

   A. $220   B. $235   C. $240   D. $250

Questions 15-22.

DIRECTIONS: Questions 15 through 22 each show in Column I the information written on five cards (lettered j, k, l, m, n) which have to be filed. You are to choose the option (lettered A, B, C, or D) in Column II which BEST represents the proper order of filing according to the information, rules, and sample question given below.

A file card record is kept of the work assignments for all the employees in a certain bureau. On each card is the employee's name, the date of work assignment, and the work assignment code number. The cards are to be filed according to the following rules:

FIRST: File in alphabetical order according to employee's name.

SECOND: When two or more cards have the same employee's name, file according to the assignment date, beginning with the earliest date.

THIRD: When two or more cards have the same employee's name and the same date, file according to the work assignment number beginning with the lowest number.

Column II shows the cards arranged in four different orders. Pick the option (A, B, C, or D) in Column II which shows the correct arrangement of the cards according to the above filing rules.

SAMPLE QUESTION

Column I
j. Cluney 4/8/02 (486503)
k. Roster 5/10/01 (246611)
l. Altool 10/15/02 (711433)
m. Cluney 12/18/02 (527610)
n. Cluney 4/8/02 (486500)

Column II
A. k, l, m, j, n
B. k, n, j, l, m
C. l, k, j, m, n
D. l, n, j, m, k

The correct way to file the cards is:
- l. Altool 10/15/02 (711433)
- n. Cluney 4/8/02 (486500)
- j. Cluney 4/8/02 (486503)
- m. Cluney 12/18/02 (527610)
- k. Roster 5/10/01 (246611)

The correct filing order is shown by the letters l, n, j, m, k. The answer to the sample question is the letter D, which appears in front of the letters l, n, j, m, k in Column II.

COLUMN I   COLUMN II

15.
- j. Smith 3/19/03 (662118)
- k. Turner 4/16/99 (481349)
- l. Terman 3/20/02 (210229)
- m. Smyth 3/20/02 (481359)
- n. Terry 5/11/01 (672128)

A. j, m, l, n, k
B. j, l, n, m, k
C. k, n, m, l, j
D. j, n, k, l, m

15._____

16.
- j. Ross 5/29/02 (396118)
- k. Rosner 5/29/02 (439281)
- l. Rose 7/19/02 (723456)
- m. Rosen 5/29/03 (829692)
- n. Ross 5/29/02 (399118)

A. l, m, k, n, j
B. m, l, k, n, j
C. l, m, k, j, n
D. m, l, j, n, k

16._____

17.
- j. Sherd 10/12/99 (552368)
- k. Snyder 11/12/99 (539286)
- l. Shindler 10/13/98 (426798)
- m. Scherld 10/12/99 (552386)
- n. Schneider 11/12/99 (798213)

A. n, m, k, j, l
B. j, m, l, k, n
C. m, k, n, j, l
D. m, n, j, l, k

17._____

18.
- j. Carter 1/16/02 (489636)
- k. Carson 2/16/01 (392671)
- l. Carter 1/16/01 (486936)
- m. Carton 3/15/00 (489639)
- n. Carson 2/16/01 (392617)

A. k, n, j, l, m
B. n, k, m, l, j
C. n, k, l, j, m
D. k, n, l, j, m

18._____

19.
- j. Thomas 3/18/99 (763182)
- k. Tompkins 3/19/00 (928439)
- l. Thomson 3/21/00 (763812)
- m. Thompson 3/18/99 (924893)
- n. Tompson 3/19/99 (928793)

A. m, l, j, k, n
B. j, m, l, k, n
C. j, l, n, m, k
D. l, m, j, n, k

19._____

20.
- j. Breit 8/10/03 (345612)
- k. Briet 5/21/00 (837543)
- l. Bright 9/18/99 (931827)
- m. Breit 3/7/98 (553984)
- n. Brent 6/14/04 (682731)

A. m, j, n, k, l
B. n, m, j, k, l
C. m, j, k, l, n
D. j, m, k, l, n

20._____

21.
- j. Roberts 10/19/02 (581932)
- k. Rogers 8/9/00 (638763)
- l. Rogerts 7/15/97 (105689)
- m. Robin 3/8/92 (287915)
- n. Rogers 4/2/04 (736921)

A. n, k, l, m, j
B. n, k, l, j, m
C. k, n, l, m, j
D. j, m, k, n, l

21._____

	COLUMN I	COLUMN II	
22.	j. Hebert 4/28/02 (719468) k. Herbert 5/8/01 (938432) l. Helbert 9/23/04 (832912) m. Herbst 7/10/03 (648599) n. Herbert 5/8/01 (487627)	A. n, k, j, m, l B. j, l, n, k, m C. l, j, k, n, m D. l, j, n, k, m	22.__

23. In order to pay its employees, the Convex Company obtained bills and coins in the following denominations:

Denomination	$20	$10	$5	$1	$.50	$.25	$.10	$.05	$.01
Number	317	122	38	73	69	47	39	25	36

What was the TOTAL amount of cash obtained?

A. $7,874.76
B. $7,878.00
C. $7,889.25
D. $7,924.35

24. H. Partridge receives a weekly gross salary (before deductions) of $596.25. Through weekly payroll deductions of $19.77, he is paying back a loan he took from his pension fund.
If other fixed weekly deductions amount to $184.14, how much pay would Mr. Partridge take home over a period of 33 weeks?

A. $11,446.92
B. $12,375.69
C. $12,947.22
D. $19,676.25

25. Mr. Robertson is a city employee enrolled in a city retirement system. He has taken out a loan from the retirement fund and is paying it back at the rate of $14.90 every two weeks. In eighteen weeks, how much money will he have paid back on the loan?

A. $268.20   B. $152.80   C. $134.10   D. $67.05

26. In 2005, the Iridor Book Company had the following expenses: rent, $6,500; overhead, $52,585; inventory, $35,700; and miscellaneous, $1,275.
If all of these expenses went up 18% in 2006, what would they TOTAL in 2006?

A. $17,290.80
B. $78,769.20
C. $96,060.00
D. $113,350.80

27. Ms. Ranier had a gross salary of $355.36, paid once every week.
If the deductions from each paycheck are $62.72, $25.13, $6.29, and $1.27, how much money would Ms. Ranier take home in four weeks?

A. $1,039.80
B. $1,421.44
C. $2,079.60
D. $2,842.88

28. Mr. Martin had a net income of $19,100 for the year. If he spent 34% on rent and household expenses, 3% on house furnishings, 25% on clothes, and 36% on food, how much was left for savings and other expenses?

A. $196.00   B. $382.00   C. $649.40   D. $1960.00

29. Mr. Elsberg can pay back a loan of $1,800 from the city employees' retirement system if   29.____
    he pays back $36.69 every two weeks for two full years.
    At the end of the two years, how much more than the original $1,800 he borrowed will
    Mr. Elsberg have paid back?

    A. $53.94   B. $107.88   C. $190.79   D. $214.76

30. Mrs. Nusbaum is a city employee, receiving a gross salary (salary before deductions) of   30.____
    $31,200. Every two weeks, the following deductions are taken out of her salary: Federal
    Income Tax, $243.96; FICA, $66.39; State Tax, $44.58; City Tax, $20.91; Health
    Insurance, $4.71.
    If Mrs.Nusbaum's salary and deductions remained the same for a full calendar year,
    what would her NET salary (gross salary less deductions) be in that year?

    A. $9,894.30   B. $21,305.70
    C. $28,118.25   D. $30,819.45

KEY (CORRECT ANSWERS)

1.	C	16.	C
2.	A	17.	D
3.	D	18.	C
4.	C	19.	B
5.	D	20.	A
6.	A	21.	D
7.	A	22.	B
8.	B	23.	A
9.	B	24.	C
10.	B	25.	C
11.	C	26.	D
12.	C	27.	A
13.	C	28.	B
14.	B	29.	B
15.	A	30.	B

EXAMINATION SECTION
TEST 1

DIRECTIONS: Each question or incomplete statement is followed by several suggested answers or completions. Select the one that BEST answers the question or completes the statement. *PRINT THE LETTER OF THE CORRECT ANSWER IN THE SPACE AT THE RIGHT.*

Questions 1-7.

DIRECTIONS: Questions 1 through 7 are to be answered on the basis of the following income statement.

    Laura Lee's Bridal Shop
    Income Statement
    For the Year Ended December 31, 2009

Revenue:		
New & Used Bridal Gowns & Accessories		$55,000
Expenses:		
Advertisement Expense	$ 2,000	
Salaries Expense	12,000	
Dry cleaning & Alterations	10,000	
Utilities	1,500	
Total Expenses		25,500
Net Income		$29,500

1. What is the period of time covered by this income statement?   1.____

    A. January-December 2008
    B. December 2009
    C. January 2008-December 2009
    D. January-December 2009

2. What is the source of the revenue?   2.____

    A. New and used bridal gowns, advertisements, salaries, dry cleaning, and utilities
    B. Advertisements, salaries, dry cleaning, alterations, and utilities
    C. New and used bridal gowns and accessories
    D. Net income

3. What is the total revenue?   3.____

    A. $25,500   B. $55,000   C. $29,500   D. $79,500

4. Which of the following are expenses?   4.____

    A. Salaries
    B. New and used bridal gowns and accessories
    C. Revenue
    D. New and used bridal gowns, advertisements, and dry cleaning

5. What are the total expenses?   5.____

    A. $55,000   B. $29,500   C. $79,500   D. $25,500

6. There is a resulting net income because
   A. total revenue and total expenses are combined
   B. net income is greater than total revenue
   C. the total revenue is greater than total expenses
   D. the total revenue is less than total expenses

7. Is this statement an interim statement?
   A. Yes, because it covers an entire accounting period
   B. No, because it covers an entire accounting period
   C. Yes, because it covers a period of less than a year
   D. No, because it covers a period of more than a year

8. What is the name of the accounting report that may show either a net profit or a net loss for an accounting period?
   A. Income statement
   B. Balance sheet
   C. Statement of capital
   D. Classified balance sheet

9. What are the two main parts of the body of the income statement?
   A. Cash and Capital
   B. Revenue and Expenses
   C. Liabilities and Capital
   D. Assets and Notes Payable

10. If total revenue exceeds total expenses for an accounting period, what is the difference called?
    A. Gross income
    B. Total liabilities
    C. Total assets
    D. Net income

11. In the body of a balance sheet, what are the three sections called?
    A. Assets and liabilities
    B. Cash, liabilities, and revenue
    C. Assets, liabilities, and capital
    D. Revenue, assets, and capital

12. What business record shows the results of the proprietor's borrowing assets from the business, usually in anticipation of profits?
    A. Proprietor's withdrawals
    B. Accounts payable
    C. Liabilities and Capital
    D. Total liabilities

Questions 13-24.

DIRECTIONS: For each transaction given for Mona's Magic Moments Hair Salon in Questions 13 through 24, identify which journal the transaction should be recorded in.

13. April 1: Mona, the owner, paid the month's rent - $600.00; check no. 356.
    A. General
    B. Cash disbursements
    C. Purchases
    D. Sales

14. April 6: the salon purchased $300.00 worth of styling products on account from Pomme de Terre Company.   14.____

   A. Cash disbursements B. General
   C. Sales   D. Purchases

15. April 8: sold $100.00 worth of hair products on account to Mrs. Angela Bray.   15.____

   A. Sales   B. Purchases
   C. Cash disbursements D. General

16. April 11: the owner, Mona Ramen, withdrew $80.00 of styling products for personal use.   16.____

   A. Sales   B. Cash receipts
   C. General   D. Cash disbursements

17. April 13: paid Pomme de Terre Company $300.00 on account; check 357.   17.____

   A. Purchases   B. Cash disbursements
   C. Cash receipts   D. General

18. April 15: cash sales to date were $4,607.00.   18.____

   A. Cash disbursements B. Purchases
   C. Sales   D. General

19. April 17: issued credit slip #17 to Mrs. Angela Bray for $25.00 for merchandise returned.   19.____

   A. Cash disbursements B. Cash receipts
   C. Sales   D. General

20. April 19: paid electric bill for $250.00; check no. 358.   20.____

   A. Cash disbursements B. Purchases
   C. General   D. Cash receipts

21. April 21: received $75.00 from Mrs. Angela Bray for balance due on account.   21.____

   A. Sales   B. Cash disbursements
   C. Cash receipts   D. Purchases

22. April 23: sold $88.00 of hair products on account to Ms. Tania Alioto.   22.____

   A. Purchases   B. Sales
   C. Cash disbursements D. Cash receipts

23. April 27: purchased $500.00 of equipment from Salon Stylings Merchandisers on account.   23.____

   A. Cash disbursements B. Sales
   C. General   D. Purchases

24. April 30: cash sales to date were $5023.00.   24.____

   A. Purchases   B. Sales
   C. Cash receipts   D. General

Questions 25-30.

DIRECTIONS: Questions 25 through 30 are to be answered on the basis of the following ledger for a barbecue take-out restaurant owned and operated by Ruby Joiner.

Cash		Accounts Receivable		Delivery Equipment	
450	150	360	170	5,000	
212	125	250	100	4,000	
328	440	165	120	3,000	
172	125	100	60		
250	70				
275	150				
325	50				

Supplies		Ruby Joiner, Capital		Accounts Payable	
40			8,200	10	600
65			2,000	15	300
30			2,097		200
25					

Ruby Joiner, Drawing		Advertising Expense		Delivery Income	
225		40			400
175		45			350
200					250
					100

Trucking Expense		Telephone Expense	
100		80	
50		40	
		20	

25. What is the balance on the Cash account shown above?
   A. 2,012.00   B. 1,110.00   C. 3,122.00   D. 902.00

26. What is the balance on the Accounts receivable account shown above?
   A. 425.00   B. 875.00   C. 450.00   D. 1315.00

27. What is the balance on the Accounts payable account shown above?
   A. 1100.00   B. 1075.00   C. 25.00   D. 1125.00

28. Which of the above accounts has a balance of 1100.00?
   A. Accounts payable
   C. Cash
   B. Delivery Income
   D. Delivery equipment

29. Which of the above accounts has a balance of 12,000.00?
   A. Ruby Joiner, Capital
   B. Cash and Accounts receivable combined
   C. Delivery equipment
   D. None of the accounts

30. If you made a balance sheet out of the information listed above, Ruby Joiner's total assets would be
   A. 14,472.00   B. 12,297.00   C. 13,392.00   D. 13,487.00

Questions 31-34.

DIRECTIONS: Questions 31 through 34 are to be answered on the basis of the following information, to be included on a checking deposit ticket.

Five $20 bills; 11 $10 bills; 6 $5 bills; 47 $1 bills; 200 half dollars; 120 quarters; 112 dimes; 320 nickels; 67 pennies. Second National Bank (73-124) check of 152.34; Bank of the Midwest (13-298) check of 68.37; Great National Bank (32-165) check of 185.06.

31. What is the TOTAL currency for this deposit?   31.____
    A. $387   B. $287   C. $444.87   D. $157.87

32. What is the TOTAL coin for this deposit?   32.____
    A. $387   B. $287   C. $444.87   D. $157.87

33. What is the check total for this deposit?   33.____
    A. $692.77   B. $406   C. $405.77   D. $850.64

34. What is the TOTAL deposit?   34.____
    A. $444.87   B. $692.77   C. $851   D. $850.64

Questions 35-37.

DIRECTIONS: Questions 35 through 37 are to be answered on the basis of the following petty cash journal.

Date	Receipt No.	To Whom Paid	For What	Acct.#	Amount
10/2	1	Anna Jones - Mail	Postage	548	13.50
10/2	2	Jim Collins	Telegram	525	5.75
10/4	3	Anna Jones - Mail	Postage	548	13.50
10/5	4	Lucky Stores	Coffee	515	7.34
10/6	5	Tom Allen	Lunch w/customer	525	11.38

35. What is the TOTAL disbursement from this fund for the time period 10/1 through 10/6?   35.____
    A. $51.47   B. $40.09   C. $61.47   D. $26.59

36. How much money was disbursed to Account #548 during the time period 10/1-10/16?   36.____
    A. $51.47   B. $26   C. $27   D. $34.34

37. If the fund began the month with a total of $100.00, what amount was left in the fund at the end of business on 10/5?   37.____
    A. $48.53   B. $59.91   C. $51.47   D. $40.09

Questions 38-40.

DIRECTIONS: Questions 38 through 40 are to be answered on the basis of the following information.

A promissory note dated December 1, 2005, bearing interest at a rate of 12% and due in 90 days, is sent to a creditor. The face value of the note is $900.

38. What is the due date of the promissory note?

   A. January 15, 2006
   B. March 1, 2006
   C. February 1, 2006
   D. December 31, 2005

39. What is the TOTAL interest that will be earned on the note?

   A. $27   B. $270   C. $108   D. $10.80

40. What interest will be earned on the note for the old accounting period (December 1-31)?

   A. $90   B. $36   C. $9   D. $3.60

KEY (CORRECT ANSWERS)

1.	D	11.	C	21.	C	31.	B
2.	C	12.	A	22.	B	32.	D
3.	B	13.	B	23.	D	33.	C
4.	A	14.	D	24.	B	34.	D
5.	D	15.	A	25.	D	35.	A
6.	C	16.	C	26.	A	36.	C
7.	B	17.	B	27.	B	37.	B
8.	A	18.	C	28.	B	38.	B
9.	B	19.	D	29.	C	39.	A
10.	D	20.	A	30.	D	40.	C

TEST 2

DIRECTIONS: Each question or incomplete statement is followed by several suggested answers or completions. Select the one that BEST answers the question or completes the statement. *PRINT THE LETTER OF THE CORRECT ANSWER IN THE SPACE AT THE RIGHT.*

Questions 1-4.

DIRECTIONS: Questions 1 through 4 are to be answered on the basis of the following information, to be included in a deposit slip.

14 twenty dollar bills	63 quarters
52 ten dollar bills	22 dimes
12 five dollar bills	44 nickels
43 one dollar bills	70 pennies

Checks: $236.34 and $129.72

1. What is the TOTAL amount of currency for this deposit?　　　　　　　　　　　1.____
    A. $923.85　　B. $1269.06　　C. $903.00　　D. $1299.91

2. What is the TOTAL amount of coin for this deposit?　　　　　　　　　　　　2.____
    A. $20.85　　B. $923.85　　C. $903.00　　D. $1299.91

3. What is the TOTAL amount of check for this deposit?　　　　　　　　　　　3.____
    A. $20.85　　B. $366.06　　C. $1299.91　　D. $903.00

4. What is the TOTAL deposit for this slip?　　　　　　　　　　　　　　　　4.____
    A. $1269.06　　B. $903.00　　C. $923.85　　D. $1289.91

Questions 5-7.

DIRECTIONS: Questions 5 through 7 are to be answered on the basis of the following information.

Angela Martinez' last check stub balance was $675.50. Her bank statement balance dated April 30 was $652.00. A $250 deposit was in transit on that date. Outstanding checks were as follows: No. 127, $65.00; No. 129, $203.50; No. 130, $50.00. The bank service charge for the nonth was $5.00.

5. What was Angela Martinez' available checkbook balance on April 30　　　　　5.____
    A. $652.00　　B. $338.50　　C. $583.50　　D. $675.50

6. In order to reconcile her checkbook balance with her bank statement balance, what must　6.____
   Angela Martinez do?

    A. Add her checkbook balance to the balance on her bank statement
    B. Subtract her checkbook balance from the balance on her bank statement

C. Ignore her checkbook balance and adopt the balance on her bank statement
D. Adjust the checkbook balance by adding deposits and debiting outstanding checks and charges

7. The check stub balance referred to in the problem refers to the

   A. last check Angela Martinez recorded in her checkbook:
   B. amount of money left in Angela Martinez' account according to her own calculations based on the checks, charges, and deposits she has written and recorded,
   C. amount of money left in Angela Martinez' account according to the bank's calculations based on the checks, charges, and deposits posted to her account,
   D. number of checks left in her checkbook

Questions 8-9.

DIRECTIONS: Questions 8 and 9 are to be answered on the basis of the following information.

Tu Nguyen, an interior designer, received his June bank statement on July 2. The balance was $622.66. His last check stub balance was $700. On comparing the two, he noticed that a deposit of $275 nade on January 30 was not included on the statement; also, a bank service charge of $4 was deducted. Outstanding checks were as follows: No. 331, $97.50; No. 332, $207; No. 335, $25.40; and No. 336, $68.97.

8. What is Nguyen's CORRECT available bank balance?

   A. $494.79   B. $897.66   C. $700.00   D. $219.79

9. The bank statement balance referred to in the problem refers to the

   A. last check Tu Nguyen recorded in his checkbook
   B. last check presented for payment to Tu Nguyen's account,
   C. amount of money left in Tu Nguyen's account according to the bank's calculations based on the checks, charges, and deposits posted to his account,
   D. amount of money left in Tu Nguyen's account based on his own calculations of the checks, charges, and deposits he has written and recorded

10. What of the following endorsements would be an example of a simple Endorsement in Blank?

    A. Pay to the Order of Joanie Anderson
    B. Joanie Anderson
    C. For deposit only; Acct. No. 12345; Joanie Anderson
    D. Without Recourse; Joanie Anderson

11. Which of the following endorsements would limit the further purpose or use of the endorsed check?

    A. Pay to the Order of Joanie Anderson
    B. Joanie Anderson
    C. For deposit only; Acct. No. 12345; Joanie Anderson,
    D. Without Recourse; Joanie Anderson

12. Which of the following endorsements would protect the endorser from legal responsibility for payment, should the drawer have insufficient funds to honor his/her own check?   12.____

    A. Pay to the Order of Joanie Anderson
    B. Joanie Anderson
    C. For deposit only; Acct. No. 12345; Joanie Anderson
    D. Without Recourse; Joanie Anderson

Questions 13-24.

DIRECTIONS: Questions 13 - 24 are to be answered on the basis of the following ledger accounts for Wheelsmith Organic Farms.

Wheelsmith Organic Farms
Ledger Accounts

Cash	Accounts Payable	Service Supplies
2006 Jan. 1 4,000	2006 Jan. 1 2,000	2006 Jan. 1 2,000

Shelley Wheelsmith, Capital	Machinery
2006 Jan. 1 11,000	2006 Jan. 1 7,000

13. Transaction #1: On January 5, Shelley Wheelsmith, the proprietor, received cash amounting to $5,000 as a result of returning machinery that had recently been purchased. What account(s) should this transaction be posted to?   13.____

    A. Cash
    B. Cash and Machinery
    C. Machinery
    D. Cash, Machinery, and Service Supplies

14. Transaction #2: On January 8, Shelley Wheelsraith, the proprietor, sent out a check for $600 in partial payment of the accounts payable.
    What account(s) should this transaction be posted to?   14.____

    A. Accounts Payable
    B. Accounts Payable and Cash
    C. Accounts Payable and Capital
    D. Cash

15. Transaction #3: On January 14, Shelley Wheelsmith, proprietor, made an additional investment in the business by contributing machinery valued at $1,500.
    What account(s) should this transaction be posted to?   15.____

    A. Machinery   B. Machinery and Capital
    C. Capital   D. Machinery and Cash

16. Transaction #4: On January 26, Shelley Wheelsmith, proprietor, purchased additional service supplies for $200. She agreed to pay the obligation in 30 days. What account(s) should this transaction be posted to?   16.____

A. Accounts Payable and Liabilities
B. Service supplies
C. Accounts Payable
D. Accounts Payable and Service supplies

17. Transaction #5: On January 31, Shelley Wheelsmith, proprietor, purchased service supplies paying cash of $50. What account(s) should this transaction be posted to?

   A. Service supplies
   B. Service supplies and Accounts Payable
   C. Cash and Service supplies
   D. Cash

18. What is the balance in the Cash account after all of these transactions are posted?
   A. $9,000   B. $1,000   C. $5,000   D. $8,350

19. What is the balance in the Machinery account after all of these transactions are posted?
   A. $7,000   B. $5,000   C. $3,500   D. $13,500

20. What is the balance in the Accounts Payable account after all of these transactions are posted?
   A. $800   B. $600   C. $2,600   D. $1,600

21. What is the balance in the Capital account after all of these transactions are posted?
   A. $12,500   B. $800   C. $11,600   D. $10,400

22. What is the balance in the Service supplies account after all of these transactions are posted?
   A. $2,000   B. $2,250   C. $750   D. $2,200

23. What are the total assets of Wheelsmith Organic Farms after these transactions have been posted?
   A. $10,600   B. $11,850   C. $14,100   D. $10,750

24. What are the total liabilities and capital for Wheelsmith Organic Farms after these transactions have been posted?
   A. $14,100   B. $12,500   C. $11,850   D. $10,600

Questions 25-28.

DIRECTIONS: Questions 25 through 28 are to be answered on the basis of the following information.

At the end of an accounting period, Andy's Framing Gallery recorded the following information: Sales, $125,225; Merchandise Inventory, December 31, 2005, $95,325; Purchases Returns and Allowances, $3,500; Merchandise Inventory, January 1, 2005, $98,725; Freight on Purchases, $2,500; Purchases, $120,000.

25. What are the net purchases for Andy's Framing Gallery during the accounting period? 25.____
    A. $120,000   B. $119,000   C. $3,500   D. $122,500

26. What is the cost of goods available for sale? 26.____
    A. $119,000   B. $98,725   C. $95,325   D. $217,725

27. What is the total cost of goods sold for this accounting period? 27.____
    A. $217,725   B. $95,325   C. $122,400   D. $125,225

28. What is the gross profit on sales for this accounting period? 28.____
    A. $2825   B. $2500   C. $125,225   D. $122,400

Questions 29-40.

DIRECTIONS: Questions 29 through 40 are to be answered on the basis of the following information.

The Joie de Vivre Co. received the promissory notes listed below during the last quarter of its calendar year:

	Date	Face Amount	Terms	Interest Rate	Date Discounted	Discount Rate
(1)	10/8	$3,600	30 days	-	10/18	9%
(2)	9/22	$8,000	60 days	6%	10/1	7%
(3)	11/15	$3,000	90 days	7%	11/20	8%

29. What is the due date for the first note? 29.____
    A. 12/31   B. 11/7   C. 12/7   D. 10/31

30. What interest will be due when the first note matures? 30.____
    A. $3   B. $3,600   C. $30   D. $0

31. What is the maturity value of the first note? 31.____
    A. $3,600   B. $3,630   C. $0   D. $3,603

32. What is the discount period for the first note? 32.____
    A. One fiscal year   B. 10 days
    C. 20 days   D. One month

33. What is the due date for the second note? 33.____
    A. 12/21   B. 11/21   C. 10/21   D. 1/21

34. What interest will be due when the second note matures? 34.____
    A. $60   B. $800.00   C. $8.00   D. $80.00

35. What is the maturity value of the second note? 35.____
    A. $8,000   B. $8,080   C. $8,800   D. $8,008

36. What is the discount period for the second note?
   A. 51 days   B. 10 days   C. 360 days   D. 60 days

37. What is the due date for the third note?
   A. 1/14   B. 12/15   C. 12/31   D. 2/13

38. What interest will be due when the third note matures?
   A. $5.25   B. $52.50   C. $525   D. $90

39. What is the maturity value of the third note?
   A. $3525   B. $3005.25   C. $3052.50   D. $3090

40. What is the discount period for the third note?
   A. 60 days   B. 85 days   C. 5 days   D. 90 days

KEY (CORRECT ANSWERS)

1.	C	11.	C	21.	A	31.	A
2.	A	12.	D	22.	B	32.	C
3.	B	13.	B	23.	C	33.	B
4.	D	14.	B	24.	A	34.	D
5.	C	15.	B	25.	B	35.	B
6.	D	16.	D	26.	D	36.	A
7.	B	17.	C	27.	C	37.	D
8.	A	18.	D	28.	A	38.	B
9.	C	19.	C	29.	B	39.	C
10.	B	20.	D	30.	D	40.	B

TEST 3

DIRECTIONS: Each question or incomplete statement is followed by several suggested answers or completions. Select the one that BEST answers the question or completes the statement. *PRINT THE LETTER OF THE CORRECT ANSWER IN THE SPACE AT THE RIGHT.*

Questions 1-8.

DIRECTIONS: Questions 1 through 8 are to be answered on the basis of the following Balance Sheet.

Laura Lee's Bridal Shop
Balance Sheet
December 31, 2009

Assets

Cash	$14,000	
Accounts Receivable	3,000	
Bridal Accessories	10,000	
Gowns and Other Inventory	30,000	
Total Assets		$57,000

Liabilities and Capital

Accounts Payable	$ 4,000	
Notes Payable	28,000	
Total Liabilities		$32,000
Laura Lee, Capital		25,000
Total Liabilities and Capital		$57,000

1. When was the balance sheet prepared?   1.____

   A. January 2010
   B. December 31, 2009
   C. After the close of the 2009 fiscal year
   D. December 1, 2009

2. How does the date on this balance sheet differ from the date on the statement of capital or income statement?   2.____

   A. It doesn't differ. The dates for each statement signify the same time period.
   B. The date on a balance sheet represents the period during which any changes indicated on the statement took place, whereas the other financial statements represent the moment in time when the statement was prepared.
   C. The date on a balance sheet represents the moment in time when the statement was prepared, whereas the other financial statements represent the period during which any changes indicated on the statement took place.
   D. The date on a balance sheet indicates an entire year, whereas the dates on the other statements indicate a single month.

3. Can Laura Lee purchase more bridal gowns for the business paying cash of $16,000?   3.____

   A. No, because the business has only $14,000 cash available
   B. Yes, because the business has $57,000 cash available
   C. Yes, because the business has $57,000 available in assets
   D. No, because the business has $57,000 in liabilities

4. What is the owner's equity of Laura Lee's Bridal Shop?
   Since total equity consists of total _____ total equity is _____.
   A. assets minus total liabilities and proprietor's capital,; $0
   B. assets minus total liabilities,; $25,000
   C. assets,; $57,000
   D. liabilities and proprietor's capital,; $57,000

5. What is the TOTAL amount of Laura Lee's claim against the total assets of the business?
   A. $57,000   B. $25,000   C. $0   D. $39,000

6. What is the amount of the creditors' claims against the assets of the business?
   A. $4,000   B. $57,000   C. $32,000   D. $28,000

7. What is the net income for the period?
   A. $57,000
   B. $0
   C. $25,000
   D. This information cannot be obtained from the balance sheet

8. What was the value of Laura Lee's ownership in this business on January 1, 2004?
   A. $25,000
   B. $57,000
   C. $14,000
   D. This information cannot be obtained from the balance sheet

Questions 9-21.

DIRECTIONS: Each of the transactions described in Questions 9 through 21 occurred within an accounting period. For each question, indicate which of the four journals the transaction would be recorded in.

9. Sale of goods on account
   A. Cash receipts   B. Cash payments
   C. General   D. Sales

10. Cash payment of a promissory note
    A. Cash payments   B. Cash receipts
    C. Sales   D. General

11. Received a credit memo from a creditor
    A. Purchases   B. General
    C. Sales   D. Cash payments

12. Sale of merchandise for cash
    A. Purchases   B. General
    C. Cash receipts   D. Cash payments

13. Received a check from a customer in partial payment of an oral agreement 13.____

    A. Purchases   B. Sales
    C. General   D. Cash receipts

14. Issued a credit memo to a customer 14.____

    A. Purchases   B. General
    C. Cash payments   D. Sales

15. Received a promissory note in place of an oral agreement from a customer 15.____

    A. General   B. Cash payments
    C. Cash receipts   D. Sales

16. Paid monthly rent 16.____

    A. General   B. Purchases
    C. Cash payments   D. Cash receipts

17. Sale of a service on credit 17.____

    A. Cash receipts   B. General
    C. Purchases   D. Sales

18. Purchase of office furniture on credit 18.____

    A. General   B. Purchases
    C. Cash payments   D. Cash receipts

19. Purchased merchandise for cash 19.____

    A. Cash payments   B. Cash receipts
    C. Sales   D. General

20. Cash refund to a customer 20.____

    A. Cash receipts   B. Sales
    C. General   D. Cash payments

21. Purchases made on credit 21.____

    A. Purchases   B. Sales
    C. Cash receipts   D. General

Questions 22-26.

DIRECTIONS: Questions 22 through 26 are to be answered on the basis of the following inventory, purchased by International Soap and Candle Traders, Inc.

700 units at $4.50, 320 units at $3.75, 550 units at $2.75, and 475 units at $1.90

22. Calculate the total price of the units that cost $4.50. 22.____

    A. $315   B. $31,500   C. $3,150   D. $2,800

23. Calculate the total price of the units that cost $3.75. 23.____

    A. $2062.50   B. $12,000   C. $120   D. $1,200

24. Calculate the total price of the units that cost $2.75.

   A. $1,512.50   B. $15,125   C. $151.25   D. $550

25. Calculate the total price of the units that cost $1.90.

   A. $90.25   B. $9025   C. $902.50   D. $475

26. Calculate the average cost per unit.

   A. $27   B. $33.10   C. $0.30   D. $3.31

27. The interest on a promissory note is recorded at which of the following times?

   A. When the debt is incurred
   B. At the end of the accounting period
   C. When the note is paid
   D. At the beginning of each month

28. The interest on a promissory note begins accruing at which of the following times?

   A. When the debt is incurred
   B. At the end of the accounting period
   C. When the note is paid
   D. At the beginning of each month

29. The maturity value of an interest-bearing note is the

   A. interest accrued on the note plus a service charge imposed by the lender
   B. interest accrued on the note
   C. face value of the note
   D. principal of the note plus interest

30. A cash receipts journal is used to record the

   A. number of cash sales a business makes
   B. number of credit sales a business makes
   C. collection of cash made by the business
   D. expenditure of cash made by the business

31. Calculate the interest on a promissory note issued for $3,000 at an interest rate of 8%, due in 360 days. (Assume a banking year of 360 days.)

   A. $300   B. $240   C. $60   D. $360

32. Calculate the total payment due for a promissory note issued for $1,000 at an interest rate of 10%, due in 90 days. (Assume a banking year of 360 days.)

   A. $25   B. $1050   C. $1000   D. $1025

33. Calculate the total payment due for a promissory note issued for $5,000 at an interest rate of 6%, due in 60 days. (Assume a banking year of 360 days.)

   A. $5,050   B. $50   C. $5,000   D. $5,300

34. Calculate the interest on a promissory note issued for $1,700 at an interest rate of 12%, due in 45 days. (Assume a banking year of 360 days.)   34.____

    A. $204   B. $1725.50   C. $25.50   D. $1904

35. Calculate the interest on a promissory note issued for $600 at an interest rate of 9%, due in 90 days. (Assume a banking year of 360 days.)   35.____

    A. $13.50   B. $135   C. $54   D. $540

KEY (CORRECT ANSWERS)

1.	B		16.	C
2.	C		17.	D
3.	A		18.	B
4.	B		19.	A
5.	B		20.	D
6.	C		21.	A
7.	D		22.	C
8.	D		23.	D
9.	D		24.	A
10.	A		25.	C
11.	B		26.	D
12.	C		27.	C
13.	D		28.	A
14.	B		29.	D
15.	A		30.	C

31.	B
32.	D
33.	A
34.	C
35.	A

OFFICE RECORD KEEPING
EXAMINATION SECTION
TEST 1

DIRECTIONS: Each question or incomplete statement is followed by several suggested answers or completions. Select the one that BEST answers the question or completes the statement. *PRINT THE LETTER OF THE CORRECT ANSWER IN THE SPACE AT THE RIGHT.*

Questions 1-5.

DIRECTIONS: Questions 1 through 5 are to be answered on the basis of the following chart to check for address and zip code errors.

    A. No errors
    B. Address only
    C. Zip code only
    D. Both

	Correct List Address	Zip Code	List to be Checked Address	Zip Code	
1.	44-A Western Avenue Bethesda, MD	65564	44-A Western Avenue Bethesda, MD	65654	1.____
2.	567 Opera Lane Jackson, MO	28218	567 Opera Lane Jacksen, MO	28218	2.____
3.	200 W. Jannine Dr. Missoula, MT	30707	200 W. Jannine Dr. Missoula, MT	30307	3.____
4.	28 Champaline Dr. Reno, NV	34101	28 Champaine Way Reno, NV	43101	4.____
5.	65156 Rodojo Parsimony, KY	44590-7326	65156 Rodojo Parsimony, KY	44590-7326	5.____

6. When alphabetized correctly, which of the following would be second?   6.____
    A. flame   B. herring   C. decadence   D. emoticon

7. Which one of the following letters is as far after E as K is before R in the alphabet?   7.____
    A. J   B. K   C. H   D. M

8. How many pairs of the following sets of numbers are exactly alike?   8.____
    134232   123456   432512   561343
    564643   432123   132439   438318

    A. 0   B. 2   C. 3   D. 4

2 (#1)

9. When alphabetized correctly, which of the following would be FOURTH? 9.____
   A. microcosm   B. natural   C. lithe   D. nature

10. When alphabetized correctly, which of the following would be THIRD? 10.____
    A. exoskeleton   B. euthanize   C. Europe   D. eurythmic

11. Which one of the following letters is as far before T as S is after I in the alphabet? 11.____
    A. j   B. K   C. M   D. N

12. How many pairs of the following sets of letters are exactly ALIKE? 12.____
    GIHEKE   GIHEKE
    KIWNEB   KWINEB
    PQMZJI   PMQZJI
    OPZIBS   OBZIBS
    PONEHE   POENHE

    A. 0   B. 1   C. 2   D. 4

13. When alphabetized correctly, which of the following would be FIRST? 13.____
    A. Catalina   B. catcher   C. caustic   D. curious

14. Which of the following letters is as far after D as U is after B in the alphabet? 14.____
    A. R   B. V   C. W   D. Z

Questions 15-19.

DIRECTIONS: Use the following information and chart to complete Questions 15 through 19.

Every theft reported to an adjuster needs to be assigned a six-letter code containing the following:

First Letter: Type of theft
Second Letter: Witnesses
Third Letter: Value of stolen item
Fourth Letter: Location
Fifth Letter: Time of theft
Sixth Letter: Elapsed between theft and report

Type of Theft:
A. Breaking and Entering
B. Retail Theft
C. Armed robbery
D. Grand Theft Auto

Witnesses
A. None
B. 1 witness
C. Multiple witnesses
D. Security camera

Location
A. Single Family Home
B. Apartment Building
C. Store
D. Office
E. Vehicle
F. Public Space (Parking Garage, Park, etc.)

Time Elapsed Between Theft and Report
A. 0-1 hour
B. 1-4 hours
C. 4-12 hours
D. 12-24 hours
E. 24 Hours

Time of Theft
A. 7 AM – 1 PM
B. 1 PM – 6 PM
C. 6 PM – 11 PM
D. 11 PM – 3 AM
E. 3 AM – 7 AM

Value of Stolen Items
A. $0-$100
B. $101-$250
C. $251-$500
D. $500-$1000
E. $1001-$5000
F. $5000 or more

15. At 9:30 PM, $175 worth of clothing was stolen from a store. The crime was reported right away by a single store associate. Which of the following would be the CORRECT code?   15.____
   A. BCCABB   B. BBBCCA   C. ACCBAB   D. CBCABB

16. A Crossover vehicle worth $4,500 was stolen from a park at approximately 6:45 AM this morning. It was reported stolen at 11:00 AM later that morning by the owner. There were no witnesses. What is the CORRECT code?   16.____
   A. DEECAF   B. CFECAE   C. DEFECA   D. DAEFEC

17. Although it was just reported, a breaking and entering occurred 5 days ago at 1:30 AM, according to security cameras that recorded the theft at the accounting firm. Although locks and doors were damaged, nothing was stolen. Which of the following would be the CORRECT code?   17.____
   A. ADDEEA   B. ADDDAE   C. ADADDE   D. ADEADE

18. Jill Wagner was held at knifepoint this morning at 11:30 AM when she was walking out of her apartment complex. The thief demanded money, and she gave him $54. She was the only witness and reported the crime immediately. Which of the following would be the CORRECT code?   18.____
   A. CBABAA   B. BBABAA   C. CBBABB   D. ABBBCA

19. An artifact worth $5,500 was stolen from the home of Chad Judea this early evening while he was out to dinner from 5:30 PM to 6 PM. When he arrived home at 6 PM, he immediately called the police. There were no witnesses. Which of the following would be the CORRECT code?   19.____
   A. AABBAF   B. AABFAF   C. AABABF   D. AAFABA

20. Diatribe means MOST NEARLY   20.____
   A. argument   B. cooperation   C. delicate   D. arrogance

21. Vitriolic means MOST NEARLY   21.____
    A. flammable   B. fearful   C. spiteful   D. asinine

22. Aplomb means MOST NEARLY   22.____
    A. self-righteous   B. respectable   C. dispirited   D. self-confidence

23. Pervicacious means MOST NEARLY   23.____
    A. rotten   B. immoral   C. stubborn   D. immortal

24. Detrimental means MOST NEARLY   24.____
    A. valuable   B. selfish   C. hopeless   D. harmful

25. Heinous means MOST NEARLY   25.____
    A. sweating   B. glorious   C. atrocious   D. moderate

KEY (CORRECT ANSWERS)

1.	C		11.	A
2.	B		12.	B
3.	C		13.	A
4.	D		14.	C
5.	A		15.	B
6.	D		16.	D
7.	B		17.	C
8.	A		18.	A
9.	D		19.	D
10.	B		20.	A

21. C
22. D
23. C
24. D
25. C

TEST 2

DIRECTIONS: Each question or incomplete statement is followed by several suggested answers or completions. Select the one that BEST answers the question or completes the statement. *PRINT THE LETTER OF THE CORRECT ANSWER IN THE SPACE AT THE RIGHT.*

Questions 1-7.

DIRECTIONS: In answering Questions 1 through 7, you will be presented with analogies (known as word relationships). Select the answer choice that BEST completes the analogy.

1. Coordinated is related to movement as speech is related to   1.____
   A. predictive   B. rapid   C. prophetic   D. articulate

2. Pottery is related to shard as wood is related to   2.____
   A. acorn   B. chair   C. smoke   D. kiln

3. Poverty is related to money as famine is related to   3.____
   A. nourishment   B. infirmity   C. illness   D. care

4. Farmland is related to arable as waterway is related to   4.____
   A. impenetrable
   B. maneuverable
   C. fertile
   D. deep

5. 19 is related to 17 as 37 is related to   5.____
   A. 39   B. 36   C. 34   D. 31

6. Cup is related to lip as bird is related to   6.____
   A. beak   B. grass   C. forest   D. bush

7. ZRYQ is related to KCJB as PWOV is related to   7.____
   A. GBHA   B. ISJT   C. ELDK   D. EOFP

Questions 8-12.

DIRECTIONS: In answering Questions 8 through 12, each of the questions has a group. Find out which one of the given alternatives will be another member of that group.

8. Springfield, Sacramento, Tallahassee   8.____
   A. Buffalo   B. Bangor   C. Pittsburgh   D. Providence

9. Lock, Shut, Fasten   9.____
   A. Window   B. Iron   C. Door   D. Block

10. Pathology, Radiology, Ophthalmology   10.____
    A. Zoology   B. Hematology   C. Geology   D. Biology

11. Karate, Jujitsu, Boxing 11.____
    A. Polo   B. Pole-vault   C. Judo   D. Swimming

12. Newspaper, Hoarding, Television 12.____
    A. Press   B. Rumor   C. Media   D. Broadcast

Questions 13-18.

DIRECTIONS: Questions 13 through 18 are to be answered on the basis of the following pie chart.

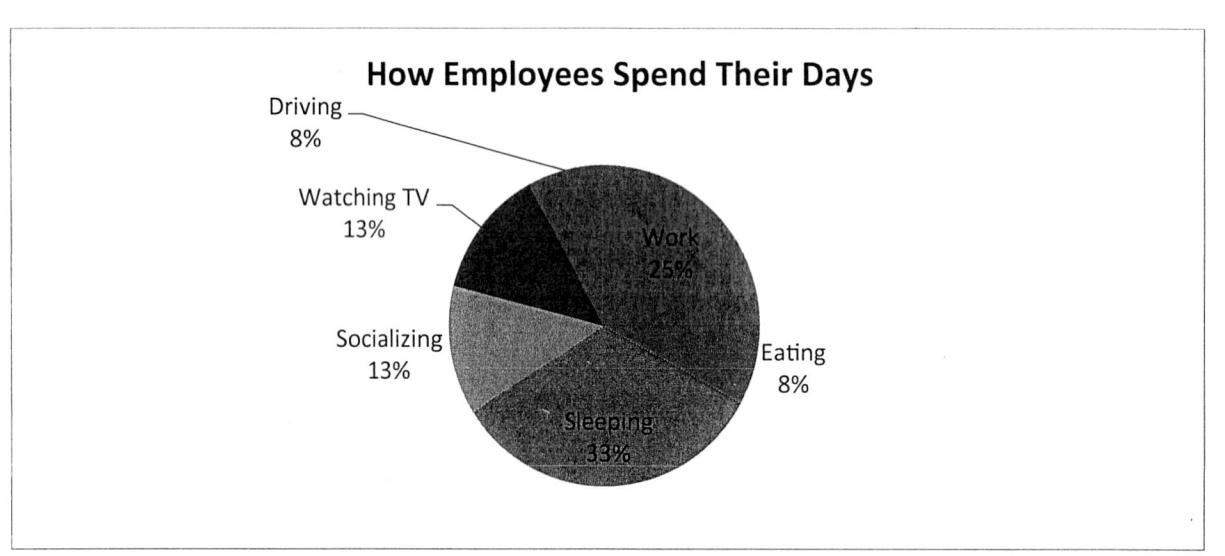

How Employees Spend Their Days

- Driving 8%
- Watching TV 13%
- Socializing 13%
- Work 25%
- Eating 8%
- Sleeping 33%

13. Approximately how many hours a day are spent eating? 13.____
    A. 2 hours   B. 5 hours   C. 1 hour   D. 30 minutes

14. According to the graph, for each 48 hour period, about how many hours are spent socializing and watching TV? 14.____
    A. 9 hours   B. 6 hours   C. 12 hours D. 3 hours

15. If an employee ate two-thirds of their meals at a restaurant, what percentage of the total day is spent eating at home? 15.____
    A. 2.5%   B. 5.3%   C. 8%   D. 1.4%

16. About how many hours a day are spent working and sleeping? 16.____
    A. 7   B. 10   C. 12   D. 14

17. Which of the following equations could be used to figure out how much time an employee spends watching TV during a week? T equals the total amount of time watching TV during the week. 17.____
    A. T = 13% x 24 x 7   B. T = 24 x 13 x 7
    C. T = 24/13% x 7   D. T = 1.3 x 7 x 24

18. How many hours a week does the average employee spend socializing? 18.____
    A. 20   B. 22   C. 23   D. 24

CODING
EXAMINATION SECTION
TEST 1

COMMENTARY

An ingenious question-type called coding, involving elements of alphabetizing, filing, name and number comparison, and evaluative judgment and application, has currently won wide acceptance in testing circles for measuring clerical aptitude and general ability, particularly on the senior (middle) grades (levels).

While the directions for this question-type usually vary in detail, the candidate is generally asked to consider groups of names, codes, and numbers, and, then, according to a given plan, to arrange codes in alphabetic order; to arrange these in numerical sequence; to re-arrange columns of names and numbers in correct order; to espy errors in coding; to choose the correct coding arrangement in consonance with the given directions and examples, etc.

This question-type appears to have few parameters in respect to form, substance, or degree of difficulty.

Accordingly, acquaintance with, and practice in the coding question is recommended for the serious candidate.

DIRECTIONS: Column I consists of serial numbers of dollar bills. Column II shows different ways of arranging the corresponding serial numbers.
The serial numbers of dollar bills in Column I begin and end with a capital letter and have an eight-digit number in between. The serial numbers in Column I are to be arranged according to the following rules:

First: In alphabetical order according to the first letter.

Second: When two or more serial numbers have the same first letter, in alphabetical order according to the last letter.

Third: When two or more serial numbers have the same first *and* last letters, in numerical order, beginning with the lowest number

The serial numbers in Column I are numbered (1) through (5) in the order in which they are listed. In Column II the numbers (1) through (5) are arranged in four different ways to show different arrangements of the corresponding serial numbers. Choose the answer in Column II in which the serial numbers are arranged according to the above rules.

Column I	Column II
1. E75044127B	A. 4, 1, 3, 2, 5
2. B96399104A	B. 4, 1, 2, 3, 5
3. B93939086A	C. 4, 3, 2, 5, 1
4. B47064465H	D. 3, 2, 5, 4, 1

In the sample question, the four serial numbers starting with B should be put before the serial number starting with E. The serial numbers starting with B and ending with A should be put before the serial number starting with B and ending with H. The three serial numbers starting with B and ending with A should be listed in numerical order, beginning with the lowest number. The correct way to arrange the serial numbers therefore is:

3. B93939086A
2. B96399104A
5. B99040922A
4. B47064465H
1. E75044127B

Since the order of arrangement is 3, 2, 5, 4, 1, the answer to the sample question is D.

2 (#1)

	Column I		Column II

1.
1. D89143888P
2. D98143838B
3. D89113883B
4. D89148338P
5. D89148388B

A. 3, 5, 2, 1, 4
B. 3, 1, 4, 5, 2
C. 4, 2, 3, 1, 5
D. 4, 1, 3, 5, 2

1. __

2.
1. W62455599E
2. W62455090F
3. W62405099E
4. V62455097F
5. V62405979E

A. 2, 4, 3, 1, 5
B. 3, 1, 5, 2, 4
C. 5, 3, 1, 4, 2
D. 5, 4, 3, 1, 2

2. __

3.
1. N74663826M
2. M74633286M
3. N76633228N
4. M76483686N
5. M74636688M

A. 2, 4, 5, 3, 1
B. 2, 5, 4, 1, 3
C. 1, 2, 5, 3, 4
D. 2, 5, 1, 4, 3

3. __

4.
1. P97560324B
2. R97663024B
3. P97503024E
4. R97563240E
5. P97652304B

A. 1, 5, 2, 3, 4
B. 3, 1, 4, 5, 2
C. 1, 5, 3, 2, 4
D. 1, 5; 2* 3, 4

4. __

5.
1. H92411165G
2. A92141465G
3. H92141165C
4. H92444165C
5. A92411465G

A. 2, 5, 3, 4, 1
B. 3, 4, 2, 5, 1
C. 3, 2, 1, 5, 4
D. 3, 1, 2, 5, 4

5. __

6.
1. X90637799S
2. N90037696S
3. Y90677369B
4. X09677693B
5. M09673699S

A. 4, 3, 5, 2, 1
B. 5, 4, 2, 1, 3
C. 5, 2, 4, 1, 3
D. 5, 2, 3, 4, 1

6. __

7.
1. K78425174L
2. K78452714C
3. K78547214N
4. K78442774C
5. K78547724M

A. 4, 2, 1, 3, 5
B. 2, 3, 5, 4, 1
C. 1, 4, 2, 3, 5
D. 4, 2, 1, 5, 3

7. __

8.
1. P18736652U
2. P18766352V
3. T17686532U
4. T17865523U
5. P18675332V

A. 1, 3, 4, 5, 2
B. 1, 5, 2, 3, 4
C. 3, 4, 5, 1, 2
D. 5, 2, 1, 3, 4

8. __

9.
1. L51138101K
2. S51138001R
3. S51188111K
4. S51183110R
5. L51188100R

A. 1, 5, 3, 2, 4
B. 1, 3, 5, 2, 4
C. 1, 5, 2, 4, 3
D. 2, 5, 1, 4, 3

9. __

	Column I		Column II	

10. 1. J28475336D A. 5, 1, 2, 3, 4
    2. T28775363D B. 4, 3, 5, 1, 2
    3. J27843566P C. 1, 5, 2, 4, 3
    4. T27834563P D. 5, 1, 3, 2, 4
    5. J28435536D

10._____

11. 1. S55126179E A. 1, 5, 2, 3, 4
    2. R55136177Q B. 3, 4, 1, 5, 2
    3. P55126177R C. 3, 5, 2, 1, 4
    4. S55126178R D. 4, 3, 1, 5, 2
    5. R55126180P

11._____

12. 1. T64217813Q A. 4, 1, 3, 2, 5
    2. I642178170 B. 2, 4, 3, 1, 5
    3. T642178180 C. 4, 1, 5, 2, 3
    4. I64217811Q D. 2, 3, 4, 1, 5
    5. T64217816Q

12._____

13. 1. B33886897B A. 5, 1, 3, 4, 2
    2. B38386882B B. 1, 2, 5, 3, 4
    3. D33389862B C. 1, 2, 5, 4, 3
    4. D33336887D D. 2, 1, 4, 5, 3
    5. B38888697D

13._____

14. 1. E11664554M A. 4, 1, 2, 5, 3
    2. F11164544M B. 2, 4, 1, 5, 3
    3. F11614455N C. 4, 2, 1, 3, 5
    4. E11665454M D. 1, 4, 2, 3, 5
    5. F16161545N

14._____

15. 1. C86611355W A. 2, 4, 1, 5, 3
    2. C68631533V B. 1, 2, 4, 3, 5
    3. G88633331W C. 1, 2, 5, 4, 3
    4. C68833515V D. 1, 2, 4, 3, 5
    5. G68833511W

15._____

16. 1. R73665312J A. 3, 2, 1, 4, 5
    2. P73685512J B. 2, 3, 5, 1, 4
    3. P73968511J C. 2, 3, 1, 5, 4
    4. R73665321K D. 3, 1, 5, 2, 4
    5. R63985211K

16._____

17. 1. X33661222U A. 1, 4, 5, 2, 3
    2. Y83961323V B. 4, 5, 1, 3, 2
    3. Y88991123V C. 4, 5, 1, 2, 3
    4. X33691233U D. 4, 1, 5, 2, 3
    5. X38691333U

17._____

	Column I	Column II	

18.
1. B22838847W
2. B28833874V
3. B22288344X
4. B28238374V
5. B28883347V

A. 4, 5, 2, 3, 1
B. 4, 2, 5, 1, 3
C. 4, 5, 2, 1, 3
D. 4, 1, 5, 2, 3

18.___

19.
1. H44477447G
2. H47444777G
3. H74777477C
4. H44747447G
5. H77747447C

A. 1, 3, 5, 4, 2
B. 3, 1, 5, 2, 4
C. 1, 4, 2, 3, 5
D. 3, 5, 1, 4, 2

19.___

20.
1. G11143447G
2. G15133388C
3. C15134378G
4. G11534477C
5. C15533337C

A. 3, 5, 1, 4, 2
B. 1, 4, 3, 2, 5
C. 5, 3, 4, 2, 1
D. 4, 3, 1, 2, 5

20.___

21.
1. J96693369F
2. J66939339F
3. J96693693E
4. J96663933E
5. J69639363F

A. 4, 3, 2, 5, 1
B. 2, 5, 4, 1, 3
C. 2, 5, 4, 3, 1
D. 3, 4, 5, 2, 1

21.___

22.
1. L15567834Z
2. P11587638Z
3. M51567688Z
4. O55578784Z
5. N53588783Z

A. 3, 1, 5, 2, 4
B. 1, 3, 5, 4, 2
C. 1, 3, 5, 2, 4
D. 3, 1, 5, 4, 2

22.___

23.
1. C83261824G
2. C78361833C
3. G83261732G
4. C88261823C
5. G83261743C

A. 2, 4, 1, 5, 3
B. 4, 2, 1, 3, 5
C. 3, 1, 5, 2, 4
D. 2, 3, 5, 1, 4

23.___

24.
1. A11710107H
2. H17110017A
3. A11170707A
4. H17170171H
5. A11710177A

A. 2, 1, 4, 3, 5
B. 3, 1, 5, 2, 4
C. 3, 4, 1, 5, 2
D. 3, 5, 1, 2, 4

24.___

25.
1. R26794821S
2. O26794821T
3. M26794827Z
4. Q26794821R
5. S26794821P

A. 3, 2, 4, 1, 5
B. 3, 4, 2, 1, 5
C. 4, 2, 1, 3, 5
D. 5, 4, 1, 2, 3

25.___

KEY (CORRECT ANSWERS)

1. A
2. D
3. B
4. C
5. A

6. C
7. D
8. B
9. A
10. D

11. C
12. B
13. B
14. D
15. A

16. C
17. A
18. B
19. D
20. C

21. A
22. B
23. A
24. D
25. A

TEST 2

DIRECTIONS: Questions 1 through 5 consist of a set of letters and numbers located under Column I. For each question, pick the answer (A, B, C, or D) located under Column II which contains *ONLY* letters and numbers that appear in the question in Column 1. *PRINT THE LETTER OF THE CORRECT ANSWER IN THE SPACE AT THE RIGHT.*

SAMPLE QUESTION

Column I	Column II
B-9-P-H-2-Z-N-8-4-M	A. B-4-C-3-R-9
	B. 4-H-P-8-6-N
	C. P-2-Z-8-M-9
	D. 4-B-N-5-E-Z

Choice C is the correct answer because P,2,Z,8,M and 9 all appear in the sample question. All the other choices have at least one letter or number that is not in the question.

	Column I		Column I	
1.	1-7-6-J-L-T-3-S-A-2	A.	J-3-S-A-7-L	1.__
		B.	T-S-A-2-6-5	
		C.	3-7-J-L-S-Z	
		D.	A-7-4-J-L-1	
2.	C-0-Q-5-3-9-H-L-2-7	A.	5-9-T-2-7-Q	2.__
		B.	3-0-6-9-L-C	
		C.	9-L-7-Q-C-3	
		D.	H-Q-4-5-9-7	
3.	P-3-B-C-5-6-0-E-1-T	A.	B-4-6-1-3-T	3.__
		B.	T-B-P-3-E-0	
		C.	5-3-0-E-B-G	
		D.	0-6-P-T-9-B	
4.	U-T-Z-2-4-S-8-6-B-3	A.	2-4-S-V-Z-3	4.__
		B.	B-Z-S-8-3-6	
		C.	4-T-U-8-L-B	
		D.	8-3-T-Z-1-2	
5.	4-D-F-G-C-6-8-3-J-L	A.	T-D-6-8-4-J	5.__
		B.	C-4-3-2-J-F	
		C.	8-3-C-5-G-6	
		D.	C-8-6-J-G-L	

Questions 6 - 12.

DIRECTIONS: Each of the questions numbered 6 through 12 consists of a long series of letters and numbers under Column I and four short series of letters and numbers under Column II. For each question, choose the short series of letters and numbers which is entirely and exactly the same as some part of the long series.

SAMPLE QUESTION:

Column I

JG13572XY89WB14

Column II

A. 1372Y8
B. XYWB14
C. 72XY89
D. J13572

In each of choices A, B, and D, one or more of the letters and numbers in the series in Column I is omitted. Only option C reproduces a segment of the series entirely and exactly. Therefore, C is the CORRECT answer to the sample question.

6. IE227FE383L4700
   A. E27FE3
   B. EF838L
   C. EL4700
   D. 83L470

7. 77J646G54NPB318
   A. NPB318
   B. J646J5
   C. 4G54NP
   D. C54NPB

8. 85887T358W24A93
   A. 858887
   B. W24A93
   C. 858W24
   D. 87T353

9. E104RY796B33H14
   A. 04RY79
   B. E14RYR
   C. 96B3H1
   D. RY7996

10. W58NP12141DE07M
    A. 8MP121
    B. W58NP1
    C. 14DEO7
    D. 12141D

11. P473R365M442V5W
    A. P47365
    B. 73P365
    C. 365M44
    D. 5X42V5

12. 865CG441V21SS59   A. 1V12SS   12.___
                              B. V21SS5
                              C. 5GC441
                              D. 894CG4

KEY (CORRECT ANSWERS)

1. A   7. A
2. C   8. B
3. B   9. A
4. B   10. D
5. D   11. C
6. D   12. B

TEST 3

DIRECTIONS : Each question from 1 to 8 consists of a set of letters and numbers. For each question, pick as your answer from the column to the right, the choice which has ONLY numbers and letters that are in the question you are answering.

To help you understand what to do, the following sample question is given:

SAMPLE :   B-9-P-H-2-Z-N-8-4-M
- A.   B-4-C-3-E-9
- B.   4-H-P-8-6-N
- C.   P-2-Z-8-M-9
- D.   4-B-N-5-E-2

Choice C is the correct answer because P, 2, Z, 8, M, 9 are in the sample question. All the other choices have at least one letter or number that is not in the question.

Questions 1 through 4 are based on Column I.

Column I

#	Question		Choice	
1.	X-8-3-I-H-9-4-G-P-U	A.	I-G-W-8-2-1	1.____
2.	4-1-2-X-U-B-9-H-7-3	B.	U-3-G-9-P-8	2.____
3.	U-I-G-2-5-4-W-P-3-B	C.	3-G-I-4-S-U	3.____
4.	3-H-7-G-4-5-I-U-8	D.	9-X-4-7-2-H	4.____

Questions 5 through 8 are based on Column II.

Column II

#	Question		Choice	
5.	L-2-9-Z-R-8-Q-Y-5-7	A.	8-R-N-3-T-Z	5.____
6.	J-L-9-N-Y-8-5-Q-Z-2	B.	2-L-R-5-7-Q	6.____
7.	T-Y-3-3-J-Q-2-N-R-Z	C.	J-2-8-Z-Y-5	7.____
8.	8-Z-7-T-N-L-1-E-R-3	D.	Z-8-9-3-L-5	8.____

KEY (CORRECT ANSWERS)

1. B
2. D
3. C
4. C
5. B
6. C
7. A
8. A

TEST 4

DIRECTIONS: Questions 1 through 5 have lines of letters and numbers. Each letter should be matched with its number in accordance with the following table:

Letter	F	R	C	A	W	L	E	N	B	T
Matching Number	0	1	2	3	4	5	6	7	8	9

From the table you can determine that the letter F has the matching number 0 below it, the letter R has the matching number 1 below it, etc.

For each question, compare each line of letters and numbers carefully to see if each letter has its correct matching number. If all the letters and numbers are matched correctly in

   none of the lines of the question, mark your answer A
   only *one* of the lines of the question, mark your answer B
   only *two* of the lines of the question, mark your answer C
   all three lines of the question, mark your answer D

	WBCR	4826
	TLBF	9580
	ATNE	3986

There is a mistake in the first line because the letter R should have its matching number 1 instead of the number 6. The second line is correct because each letter shown has the correct matching number.
There is a mistake in the third line because the letter N should have the matching number 7 instead of the number 8. Since all the letters and numbers are matched correctly in only one of the lines in the sample, the correct answer is B.

1.   EBCT   6829   1.____
          ATWR   3961
          NLBW   7584

2.   RNCT   1729   2.____
          LNCR   5728
          WAEB   5368

3.   STWB   7948   3.____
          RABL   1385
          TAEF   9360

4.   LWRB   5417   4.____
          RLWN   1647
          CBWA   2843

5.   ABTC   3792
          WCER   5261
          AWCN   3417

KEY (CORRECT ANSWERS)

1. C
2. B
3. D
4. B
5. A

TEST 5

DIRECTIONS: Assume that each of the capital letters in the table below represents the name of an employee enrolled in the city employees retirement system. The number directly beneath the letter represents the agency for which the employee works, and the small letter directly beneath represents the code for the employees account.

Name of Employee	L	O	T	Q	A	M	R	N	C
Agency	3	4	5	9	8	7	2	1	6
Account Code	r	f	b	i	d	t	g	e	n

In each of the following Questions 1 through 10, the agency code numbers and the account code letters in Columns 2 and 3 should correspond to the capital letters in Column 1 and should be in the same consecutive order. For each question, look at each column carefully and mark your answer as follows:

If there are one or more errors in *Column 2 only,* mark your answer A,

If there are one or more errors in *Column 3 only,* mark your answer B.

If there are one or more errors in Column 2 *and* one or more errors in Column 3, mark your answer C.

If there are NO errors in either column, mark your answer D,

The following sample question is given to help you understand the procedure.

Column 1	Column 2	Column 3
T Q L M O C	5 8 3 7 4 6	b i r t f n

In Column 2, the second agency code number (corresponding to letter Q) should be "9", not "8". Column 3 is coded correctly to Column 1. Since there is an error only in Column 2, the correct answer is A.

	Column 1	Column 2	Column 3	
1.	Q L N R C A	9 3 1 2 6 8	i f e g n d	1.____
2.	N R M O T C	1 2 7 5 4 6	e g f t b n	2.____
3.	R C T A L M	2 6 5 8 3 7	g n d b r t	3.____
4.	T A M L O N	5 7 8 3 4 1	b d t r f e	4.____
5.	A N T O R M	8 1 5 4 2 7	d e b i g t	5.____
6.	M R A L O N	7 2 8 3 4 1	t g d r f e	6.____
7.	C T N Q R O	6 5 7 9 2 4	n d e i g f	7.____
8.	Q M R O T A	9 7 2 4 5 8	i t g f b d	8.____
9.	R Q M C O L	2 9 7 4 6 3	g i t n f r	9.____
10.	N O M R T Q	1 4 7 2 5 9	e f t g b i	10.____

KEY (CORRECT ANSWERS)

1. D
2. C
3. B
4. A
5. B
6. D
7. C
8. D
9. A
10. D

TEST 6

DIRECTIONS: Each of Questions 1 through 6 consists of three lines of code letters and numbers. The numbers on each line should correspond to the code letters on the same line in accordance with the table below.

Code Letter	D	Y	K	L	P	U	S	R	A	E
Corresponding Number	0	1	2	3	4	5	6	7	8	9

On some of the lines an error exists in the coding. Compare the letters and numbers in each question carefully. If you find an error or errors on
   only *one* of the lines in the question, mark your answer A;
   any *two* lines in the question, mark your answer B;
   all *three* lines in the question, mark your answer C;
   none of the lines in the question, mark your answer D.

SAMPLE QUESTION
KSRYELD - 2671930
SAPUEKL - 6845913
RYKADLP - 5128034

In the above sample, the first line is correct since each code letter listed has the correct corresponding number. On the second line, an error exists because code letter K should have number 2 instead of number 1. On the third line, an error exists because the code letter R should have the number 7 instead of the number 5. Since there are errors on two of the three lines, the correct answer is B.

Now answer the following questions, using the same procedure.

1. YPUSRLD - 1456730
   UPSAEDY - 5648901
   PREYDKS - 4791026

2. AERLPUS - 8973456
   DKLYDPA - 0231048
   UKLDREP - 5230794

3. DAPUSLA - 0845683
   YKLDLPS - 1230356
   PUSKYDE - 4562101

4. LRPUPDL - 3745403
   SUPLEDR - 6543907
   PKEYDLU - 4291025

5. KEYDESR - 2910967
   PRSALEY - 4678391
   LSRAYSK - 3687162

6. YESREYL - 1967913
   PLPRAKY - 4346821
   YLPSRDU - 1346705

1.____
2.____
3.____
4.____
5.____
6.____

TEST 6

KEY (CORRECT ANSWERS)

1. A
2. D
3. C
4. A
5. B
6. A

ARITHMETICAL REASONING
EXAMINATION SECTION
TEST 1

DIRECTIONS: Each question or incomplete statement is followed by several suggested answers or completions. Select the one that BEST answers the question or completes the statement. *PRINT THE LETTER OF THE CORRECT ANSWER IN THE SPACE AT THE RIGHT.*

1. The ABC Corporation had a gross income of $125,500.00 in 2004. Of this, it paid 60% for overhead.
   If the gross income for 2005 increased by $6,500 and the cost of overhead increased to. 61% of gross income, how much MORE did it pay for overhead in 2005 than in 2004?

   A. $1,320   B. $5,220   C. $7,530   D. $8,052

   1._____

2. After one year, Mr. Richards paid back a total of $16,950 as payment for a $15,000 loan. All the money paid over $15,000 was simple interest.
   The interest charge was MOST NEARLY

   A. 13%   B. 11%   C. 9%   D. 7%

   2._____

3. A checking account has a balance of $253.36.
   If deposits of $36.95, $210.23, and $7.34 and withdrawals of $117.35, $23.37, and $15.98 are made, what is the NEW balance of the account?

   A. $155.54   B. $351.18   C. $364.58   D. $664.58

   3._____

4. In 2004, The W Realty Company spent 27% of its income on rent.
   If it earned $97,254 in 2004, the amount it paid for rent was

   A. $26,258.58   B. $26,348.58
   C. $27,248.58   D. $27,358.58

   4._____

5. Six percent simple annual interest on $2,436.18 is MOST NEARLY

   A. $145.08   B. $145.17   C. $146.08   D. $146.17

   5._____

6. H. Partridge receives a weekly gross salary (before deductions) of $397.50. Through weekly payroll deductions of $13.18, he is paying back a loan he took from his pension fund.
   If other fixed weekly deductions amount to $122.76, how much pay would Mr. Partridge take home over a period of 33 weeks?

   A. $7,631.28   B. $8,250.46   C. $8,631.48   D. $13,117.50

   6._____

7. Mr. Robertson is a city employee enrolled in a city retirement system. He has taken out a loan from the retirement fund and is paying it back at the rate of $14.90 every two weeks. In eighteen weeks, how much money will he have paid back on the loan?

   A. $268.20   B. $152.80   C. $134.10   D. $67.05

   7._____

8. In 2004, The Iridor Book Company had the following expenses: rent, $6,500; overhead, $52,585; inventory, $35,700; and miscellaneous, $1,275.
   If all of these expenses went up 18% in 2005, what would they TOTAL in 2005?

   A. $17,290.80
   B. $78,769.20
   C. $96,060.00
   D. $113,350.80

9. Ms. Ranier had a gross salary of $710.72 paid once every two weeks.
   If the deductions from each paycheck are $125.44, $50.26, $12.58, and $2.54, how much money would Ms. Ranier take home in eight weeks?

   A. $2,079.60   B. $2,842.88   C. $4,159.20   D. $5,685.76

10. Mr. Martin had a net income of $95,500 in 2004.
    If he spent 34% on rent and household expenses, 3% on house furnishings, 25% on clothes, and 36% on food, how much was left for savings and other expenses?

    A. $980   B. $1,910   C. $3,247   D. $9,800

11. Mr. Elsberg can pay back a loan of $1,800 from the city employees' retirement system if he pays back $36.69 every two weeks for two full years.
    At the end of the two years, how much more than the original $1,800 he borrowed will Mr. Elsberg have paid back?

    A. $53.94   B. $107.88   C. $190.79   D. $214.76

12. Mr. Nusbaum is a city employee receiving a gross salary (salary before deductions) of $20,800. Every two weeks the following deductions are taken out of his salary: Federal Income Tax, $162.84; FICA, $44.26; State Tax, $29.72; City Tax, $13.94; Health Insurance, $3.14.
    If Mr. Nusbaum's salary and deductions remained the same for a full calendar year, what would his net salary (gross salary less deductions) be in that year?

    A. $6,596.20
    B. $14,198.60
    C. $18,745.50
    D. $20,546.30

13. Add: 8936
         7821
         8953
         4297
         9785
         6579

    A. 45,371   B. 45,381   C. 46,371   D. 46,381

14. Multiply: 987
              867

    A. 854,609   B. 854,729   C. 855,709   D. 855,729

15. Divide: 59)321439.0

    A. 5438.1   B. 5447.1   C. 5448.1   D. 5457.1

16. Divide: .052)̄721͞ 16._____

    A. 12,648.0   B. 12,648.1   C. 12,649.0   D. 12,649.1

17. If the total number of employees in one city agency increased from 1,927 to 2,006 during a certain year, the percentage increase in the number of employees for that year is MOST NEARLY 17._____

    A. 4%   B. 5%   C. 6%   D. 7%

18. During a single fiscal year, which totaled 248 workdays, one account clerk verified 1,488 purchase vouchers. Assuming a normal work week of five days, what is the AVERAGE number of vouchers verified by the account clerk in a one-week period during this fiscal year? 18._____

    A. 25   B. 30   C. 35   D. 40

19. Multiplying a number by .75 is the same as 19._____

    A. multiplying it by 2/3   B. dividing it by 2/3
    C. multiplying it by 3/4   D. dividing it by 3/4

20. In City Agency A, 2/3 of the employees are enrolled in a retirement system. City Agency B has the same number of employees as Agency A, and 60% of these are enrolled in a retirement system.
    If Agency A has a total of 660 employees, how many MORE employees does it have enrolled in a retirement system than does Agency B? 20._____

    A. 36   B. 44   C. 56   D. 66

21. Net worth is equal to assets minus liabilities.
    If, at the end of 2003, a textile company had assets of $98,695.83 and liabilities of $59,238.29, what was its net worth? 21._____

    A. $38,478.54   B. $38,488.64
    C. $39,457.54   D. $48,557.54

22. Mr. Martin's assets consist of the following: 22._____
    Cash on hand $ 5,233.74
    Automobile   3,206.09
    Furniture   4,925.00
    Government Bonds   5,500.00
    House   36,690.85
    What are his TOTAL assets?

    A. $54,545.68   B. $54,455.68
    C. $55,455.68   D. $55,555.68

23. If Mr. Mitchell has $627.04 in his checking account and then writes three checks for $241.75, $13.24, and $102.97, what will be his new balance? 23._____

    A. $257.88   B. $269.08   C. $357.96   D. $369.96

24. An employee's net pay is equal to his total earnings less all deductions. 24.___
If an employee's total earnings in a pay period are $497.05, what is his net pay if he has the following deductions: Federal income tax, $90.32; FICA, $28.74; State tax, $18.79; City tax, $7.25; Pension, $1.88?

    A. $351.17   B. $351.07   C. $350.17   D. $350.07

25. A petty cash fund had an opening balance of $85.75 on December 1. Expenditures of 25.___
$23.00, $15.65, $5.23, $14.75, and $26.38 were made out of this fund during the first 14 days of the month. Then, on December 17, another $38.50 was added to the fund.
If additional expenditures of $17.18, $3.29, and $11.64 were made during the remainder of the month, what was the FINAL balance of the petty cash fund at the end of December?

    A. $6.93   B. $7.13   C. $46.51   D. $91.40

KEY (CORRECT ANSWERS)

1. B		11. B	
2. A		12. B	
3. B		13. C	
4. A		14. D	
5. D		15. C	
6. C		16. D	
7. C		17. A	
8. D		18. B	
9. A		19. C	
10. B		20. B	

21. C
22. D
23. B
24. D
25. B

SOLUTIONS TO PROBLEMS

1. ($132,000)(.61)-($125,500)(.60) = $5220

2. Interest = $1950. As a percent, $1950÷15,000 = 13%

3. New balance = $253.36 + $36.95 + $210.23 + $7.34 - $117.35 -$23.37 - $15.98 = $351.18

4. Rent = ($97,254)(.27) = $26,258.58

5. ($2436.18)(.06) ≈ $146.17

6. ($397.50-$13.18-$122.76)(33) = $8631.48

7. ($14.90)($\frac{18}{2}$) = $134.10

8. ($6500+$52,585+$35,700+$1275)(1.18) = $113,350.80

9. ($710.72-$125.44-$50.26-$12.58-$2.54)($\frac{8}{2}$) = $2079.60

10. (1-.34-.03-.25-.36)($95,500) = $1910

11. ($36.69)(52) - $1800 = $107.88

12. $20,800 - (26)($162.84+$44.26+$29.72+$13.94+$3.14) = $14,198.60

13. 8936 + 7821 + 8953 + 4297 + 9785 + 6579 = 46,371

14. (987)(867) = 855,729

15. 321,439÷59 ≈ 5448.1

16. 721 ÷ .057 ≈ 12,649.1

17. (2006-1927)÷ 1927 ≈ 4%

18. Let x=number of vouchers. Then, $\frac{x}{5}=\frac{1488}{248}$. Solving, x=30

19. Multiplying by .75 is equivalent to multiplying by $\frac{3}{4}$

20. (660)($\frac{2}{3}$) - (660)(.60) = 44

21. Net worth = $98,695.83 - $59,238.29 = $39,457.54

22. Total assets = $5233.74 + $3206.09 + $4925.00 + $5500.00 + $36,690.85 = $55,555.68

23. New balance = $627.04 - $241.75 - $13.24 - $102.97 = $269.08

24. Net pay = $497.05 - $90.32 - $28,74 - $18.79 - $7.25 - $1.88 = $350.07

25. Final balance = $85.75 - $23.00 - $15.65 - $5.23 - $14.75 - $26.38 + $38.50 - $17.18 - $3.29 - $11.64 = $7.13

TEST 2

DIRECTIONS: Each question or incomplete statement is followed by several suggested answers or completions. Select the one that BEST answers the question or completes the statement. *PRINT THE LETTER OF THE CORRECT ANSWER IN THE SPACE AT THE RIGHT.*

1. The formula for computing base salary is: Earnings equals base gross plus additional gross.
   If an employee's earnings during a particular period are in the amounts of $597.45, $535.92, $639.91, and $552.83, and his base gross salary is $525.50 per paycheck, what is the TOTAL of the additional gross earned by the employee during that period?

   A. $224.11   B. $224.21   C. $224.51   D. $244.11

   1._____

2. If a lump sum death benefit is paid by the retirement system in an amount equal to 3/7 of an employee's last yearly salary of $13,486.50, the amount of the death benefit paid is MOST NEARLY

   A. $5,749.29   B. $5,759.92   C. $5,779.92   D. $5,977.29

   2._____

3. Suppose that a member has paid 15 installments on a 28-installment loan.
   The percentage of the number of installments paid to the retirement system is

   A. 53.57%   B. 53.97%   C. 54.57%   D. 55.37%

   3._____

4. If an employee takes a 1-month vacation during a calendar year, the percentage of the year during which he works is MOST NEARLY

   A. 90.9%   B. 91.3%   C. 91.6%   D. 92.1%

   4._____

5. Suppose that an employee took a leave of absence totaling 7 months during a calendar year.
   Assuming the employee did not take any vacation time during the remainder of that year, the percentage of the year in which he worked is MOST NEARLY

   A. 41.7%   B. 43.3%   C. 46.5%   D. 47.1%

   5._____

6. A member has borrowed $4,725 from her funds in the retirement system.
   If $3,213 has been repaid, the percentage of the loan which is still outstanding is MOST NEARLY

   A. 16%   B. 32%   C. 48%   D. 68%

   6._____

7. If an employee worked only 24 weeks during the year because of illness, the portion of the year he was out of work was MOST NEARLY

   A. 46%   B. 48%   C. 51%   D. 54%

   7._____

8. If an employee purchased credit for a 16-week period of service which he had prior to rejoining the retirement system, the percentage of a year he purchased credit for was MOST NEARLY

   A. 27.9%   B. 28.8%   C. 30.7%   D. 33.3%

   8._____

9. If an employee contributes 2/11 of his yearly salary to his pension fund account, the percentage of his yearly salary which he contributes is MOST NEARLY

   A. 17.9%   B. 18.2%   C. 18.4%   D. 19.0%

10. In 2005, the maximum amount of income from which social security tax could be withheld (base salary) was $70,500. In 2007, the base salary was $82,500.
    The 2007 base salary represents a percentage increase over the 2005 base salary of approximately

    A. 15%   B. 16%   C. 17%   D. 18%

11. If 17.5% of an employee's salary is withheld for taxes, the one of the following which is the fraction of the salary withheld is

    A. 3/20   B. 8/35   C. 7/40   D. 4/25

12. If a person withdraws 42% of the funds from his account with the retirement system, the remaining balance represents a fraction of MOST NEARLY

    A. 7/13   B. 5/9   C. 7/12   D. 4/7

13. A property decreases in value from $45,000 to $35,000. The percent of decrease is MOST NEARLY

    A. 20.5%   B. 22.2%   C. 25.0%   D. 28.6%

14. The fraction $\frac{487}{101326}$ expressed as a decimal is MOST NEARLY

    A. .0482   B. .00481   C. .0049   D. .00392

15. The reciprocal of the sum of 2/3 and 1/6 can be expressed as

    A. 0.83   B. 1.20   C. 1.25   D. 1.50

16. Total land and building costs for a new commercial property equal $50 per square foot. If the investors expect a 10 percent return on their costs, and if total operating expenses average 5 percent of total costs, annual gross rentals per square foot must be AT LEAST

    A. $7.50   B. $8.50   C. $10.00   D. $12.00

17. The formula for computing the amount of annual deposit in a compound interest bearing account to provide a lump sum at the end of a period of years is $X = \frac{r \cdot L}{(1+r)^{n-1}}$ (X is the amount of annual deposit, r is the rate of interest, and n is the number of years) and L = lump sum)
    Using the formula, the annual amount of the deposit at the end of each year to accumulate to $20,000 at the end of 3 years with interest at 2 percent on annual balances is

    A. $6,120.00   B. $6,203.33   C. $6,535.09   D. $6,666.66

18. An investor sold two properties at $150,000 each. On one he made a 25 percent profit. On the other he suffered a 25 percent loss.
    The NET result of his sales was

    A. neither a gain nor a loss
    B. a $20,000 loss
    C. a $75,000 gain
    D. a $75,000 loss

19. A contractor decides to install a chain fence covering the perimeter of a parcel 75 feet wide and 112 feet in depth.
    Which one of the following represents the number of feet to be covered?

    A. 187   B. 364   C. 374   D. 8,400

20. A builder estimates he can build an average of 4 1/2 one-family homes to an acre. There are 640 acres to one square mile.
    Which one of the following CORRECTLY represents the number of one-family homes the builder would estimate he can build on one square mile?

    A. 1,280   B. 1,920   C. 2,560   D. 2,880

21. $.01059 deposited at 7 percent interest will yield $1.00 in 30 years.
    If a person deposited $1,059 at 7 percent interest on April 1, 1974, which one of the following amounts would represent the worth of this deposit on March 31, 2004?

    A. $100   B. $1,000   C. $10,000   D. $100,000

22. A building has an economic life of forty years. Assuming the building depreciates at a constant annual rate, which one of the following CORRECTLY represents the yearly percentage of depreciation?

    A. 2.0%   B. 2.5%   C. 5.0%   D. 7.0%

23. A building produces a gross income of $200,000 with a net income of $20,000, before mortgage charges and capital recapture. The owner is able to increase the gross income 5 percent without a corresponding increase in operating costs.
    The effect upon the net income will be an INCREASE of

    A. 5%   B. 10%   C. 12.5%   D. 50%

24. The present value of $1.00 not payable for 8 years, and at 10 percent interest, is $.4665.
    Which of the following amounts represents the PRESENT value of $1,000 payable 8 years hence at 10 percent interest?

    A. $46.65   B. $466.50   C. $4,665.00   D. $46,650.00

25. The amount of real property taxes to be levied by a city is $100 million. The assessment roll subject to taxation shows an assessed valuation of $2 billion.
    Which one of the following tax rates CORRECTLY represents the tax rate to be levied per $100 of assessed valuation?

    A. $.50   B. $5.00   C. $50.00   D. $500.00

KEY (CORRECT ANSWERS)

1.	A	11.	C
2.	C	12.	C
3.	A	13.	B
4.	C	14.	B
5.	A	15.	B
6.	B	16.	A
7.	D	17.	C
8.	C	18.	B
9.	B	19.	C
10.	C	20.	D

21. D
22. B
23. D
24. B
25. B

SOLUTIONS TO PROBLEMS

1. $597.45 + $535.92 + $639.91 + $552.83 = $2326.11 Then, $2326.11 - (4)($525.50) = $224.11

2. Death benefit = ($13,486.50)($\frac{3}{7}$) ≈ $5779.92

3. $\frac{15}{28}$ ≈ 53.57%

4. $\frac{11}{12}$ ≈ 91.6% (closer to 91.7%)

5. $\frac{5}{12}$ ≈ 41.7%

6. ($4725-$3213) ÷ $4725 = 32%

7. $\frac{28}{52}$ ≈ 54%

8. $\frac{16}{52}$ ≈ 30.7% (closer to 30.8%)

9. $\frac{2}{11}$ ≈ 18.2%

10. ($82,500-$70,500) ÷ $70,500 = 17%

11. 17.5% = $\frac{175}{1000}$ = $\frac{7}{40}$

12. 100% - 42% = 58% = $\frac{58}{100}$ = $\frac{29}{50}$, closest to $\frac{7}{12}$ in selections

13. $\frac{\$10,000}{\$45,000}$ ≈ 22.2%

14. 487/101,326 ≈ .00481

15. $\dfrac{2}{3}+\dfrac{1}{6}=\dfrac{5}{6}$ Then, $1\div\dfrac{5}{6}=\dfrac{6}{5}=1.20$

16. $(.15)(\$50) = \$7.50$

17. $x = (.02)(\$20,000)/[(1+.02)^3-1] = 400 \div .061208 \approx \$6535.09$

18. Sold 150,000, 25% loss = paid 200,000, loss of 50,000 Sold 150,000, 25% profit = paid 120,000, profit of 30,000 - 50,000 + 30,000 = -20,000 (loss)

19. Perimeter = (2)(75) + (2)(112) = 374 ft.

20. (640)(4 1/2) = 2880 homes

21. $(1\div.01059)(1059) = \$100,000$

22. $1 \div 40 = .025 = 2.5\%$

23. New gross income = ($200,000)(X1.05) = $210,000.
    Then, ($210,000-$200,000) ÷ $20,000 = 50%

24. Let x = present value of $1000. Then, $\dfrac{\$1.00}{\$.4665}=\dfrac{\$1000}{x}$
    Solving, x = $466.50

25. Let x = tax rate. Then, $\dfrac{\$100,000,000}{\$2,000,000,000}=\dfrac{x}{\$100}$
    Solving, x = $5.00

TEST 3

DIRECTIONS: Each question or incomplete statement is followed by several suggested answers or completions. Select the one that BEST answers the question or completes the statement. *PRINT THE LETTER OF THE CORRECT ANSWER IN THE SPACE AT THE RIGHT.*

1. It is found that for the past three years the average weekly number of inspections per inspector ranged from 20 inspections to 40 inspections.
   On the basis of this information, it is MOST reasonable to conclude that

   A. on the average, 30 inspections per week were made
   B. the average weekly number of inspections never fell below 20
   C. the performance of inspectors deteriorated over the three-year period
   D. the range in average weekly inspections was 60

   1._____

Questions 2-4.

DIRECTIONS: Questions 2 through 4 are to be answered on the basis of the following information.

The number of students admitted to University X in 2004 from High School Y was 268 students. This represented 13.7 percent of University X's entering freshman classes. In 2005, it is expected that University X will admit 591 students from High School Y, which is expected to represent 19.4 percent of the 2005 entering freshman classes of University X. t

2. Which of the following is the CLOSEST estimate of the size of University X's expected 2005 entering freshman classes?
   _____ students.

   A. 2,000   B. 2,500   C. 3,000   D. 3,500

   2._____

3. Of the following, the expected percentage of increase from 2004 to 2005 in the number of students graduating from High School Y and entering University X as freshmen is MOST NEARLY

   A. 5.7%   B. 20%   C. 45%   D. 120%

   3._____

4. Assume that the cost of processing each freshman admission to University X from High School Y in 2004 was an average of $28. Also, that this was 1/3 more than the average cost of processing each of the other 2004 freshman admissions to University X. Then, the one of the following that MOST closely shows the total processing cost of all 2004 freshman admissions to University X is

   A. $6,500   B. $20,000   C. $30,000   D. $40,000

   4._____

5. Assume that during the fiscal year 2005-2006, a bureau produced 20% more work units than it produced in the fiscal year 2004-2005. Also assume that during the fiscal year 2005-2006 that bureau's staff was 20% smaller than it was in the fiscal year 2004-2005. On the basis of this information, it would be MOST proper to conclude that the number of work units produced per staff member in that bureau in the fiscal year 2005-2006 exceeded the number of work units produced per staff member in that bureau in the fiscal year 2004-2005 by which one of the following percentages?

   A. 20%   B. 25%   C. 40%   D. 50%

   5._____

6. Assume that during the following five fiscal years (FY), a bureau has received the following appropriations:
   FY 2002-2003 - $200,000
   FY 2003-2004 - $240,000
   FY 2004-2005 - $280,000
   FY 2005-2006 - $390,000
   FY 2006-2007 - $505,000

   The bureau's appropriation for which one of the following fiscal years showed the LARGEST percentage of increase over the bureau's appropriation for the immediately previous fiscal year?

   A. FY 2003-2004 B. FY 2004-2005
   C. FY 2005-2006 D. FY 2006-2007

7. Assume that the number of buses (U_t) required for a given line-haul system serving the Central Business District depends upon roundtrip time (t), capacity of bus (c), and the total number of people to be moved in a peak hour (P) in the major direction, i.e., in the morning and out in the evening.
   The formula for the number of buses required is

   A. $U_t = Ptc$ B. $U_t = \dfrac{tP}{c}$ C. $U_t = \dfrac{cP}{t}$ D. $U_t = \dfrac{ct}{P}$

8. The area, in blocks, that can be served by a single stop for any maximum walking distance is given by the following formula: $a = 2w^2$. In this formula, a = the area served by a stop, and w = maximum walking distance.
   If people will tolerate a walk of up to three blocks, how many stops would be needed to service an area of 288 square blocks?

   A. 9   B. 16   C. 18   D. 27

Questions 9-11.

DIRECTIONS: Questions 9 through 11 are to be answered on the basis of the following information.

In 2006, a police precinct records 456 cases of car thefts which is 22.6 percent of all grand larcenies. In 2007, there were 560 such cases, which constituted 35% of the broader category.

9. The number of crimes in the broader category in 2007 was MOST NEARLY

   A. 1,600   B. 1,700   C. 1,960   D. 2,800

10. The change from 2006 to 2007 in the number of crimes in the broader category represented MOST NEARLY a

    A. 2.5% decrease   B. 10.1% increase
    C. 12.5% increase   D. 20% decrease

11. In 2007, one out of every 6 of these crimes was solved. This represents MOST NEARLY what percentage of the total number of crimes in the broader category that year?

    A. 5.8   B. 6   C. 9.3   D. 12

12. Assume that a maintenance shop does 5 brake jobs to every 3 front-end jobs. It does 8,000 jobs altogether in a 240-day year. In one day, one worker can do 3 front-end jobs or 4 brake jobs.
About how many workers will be needed in the shop?

    A. 3 B. 5 C. 10 D. 18

13. Assume that the price of a certain item declines by 6% one year, and then increases by 5 and 10 percent, respectively, during the next two years.
What is the OVERALL increase in price over the three-year period?

    A. 4.2 B. 6 C. 8.6 D. 10.1

14. After finding the total percent change in a price (TO over a three-year period, as in the preceding question, one could compute the average annual percent change in the price by using the formula

    A. $(1 + TC)^{1/3}$
    B. $\dfrac{(1 + TC)}{3}$
    C. $(1 + TC)^{1/3 - 1}$
    D. $\dfrac{1}{(1+TC)^{1/3}-1}$

15. 357 is 6% of

    A. 2,142 B. 5,950 C. 4,140 D. 5,900

16. In 2002, a department bought n pieces of a certain supply item for a total of $x. In 2003, the department bought k percent fewer of the item but had to pay a total of g percent more for it.
Which of the following formulas is CORRECT for determining the average price per item in 2003?

    A. $100\dfrac{xg}{nk}$
    B. $\dfrac{x(100+g)}{n(100-k)}$
    C. $\dfrac{x(100-g)}{n(100+k)}$
    D. $\dfrac{x}{n}-100\dfrac{g}{k}$

17. A sample of 18 income tax returns, each with 4 personal exemptions, is taken for 2001 and for 2002. The breakdown is as follows in terms of income:

Average gross income (in thousands)	Number of returns 2001	2002
40	6	2
80	10	11
120	2	5

    There is a personal deduction per exemption of $500.
    There are no other expense deductions. In addition, there is an exclusion of $3,000 for incomes less than $50,000 and $2,000 for incomes from $50,000 to $99,999.99.
    From $100,000 upward there is no exclusion.

    The average net taxable income for the samples in thousands) for 2001 is MOST NEARLY

    A. $67 B. $85 C. $10 D. $128

4 (#3)

18. In the preceding question, the increase in average net taxable income for the sample (in thousands) between 2001 and 2002 is

    A. 16   B. 20   C. 24   D. 34

19. Assume that supervisor S has four subordinates - A, B, C, and D.
    The MAXIMUM number of relationships, assuming that all combinations are included, that can exist between S and his subordinates is

    A. 28   B. 15   C. 7   D. 4

20. If the workmen's compensation insurance rate for clerical workers is 93 cents per $100 of wages, the total premium paid by a city whose clerical staff earns $8,765,000 is MOST NEARLY

    A. $8,150   B. $81,515   C. $87,650   D. $93,765

21. Assume that a budget of $3,240,000,000 for the fiscal year beginning July 1, 2003 has been approved. A city sales tax is expected to provide $1,100,000,000; licenses, fees and sundry revenues are expected to yield $121,600,000; the balance is to be raised from property taxes. A tax equalization board has appraised all property in the city at a fair value of $42,500,000,000. The council wishes to assess property at 60% of its fair value.
    The tax rate would need to be MOST NEARLY _____ per $100 of assessed value.

    A. $12.70   B. $10.65   C. $7.90   D. $4.00

22. Men's white linen handkerchiefs cost $12.90 for 3. The cost per dozen handkerchiefs is

    A. $77.40   B. $38.70   C. $144.80   D. $51.60

23. Assume that it is necessary to partition a room measuring 40 feet by 20 feet into eight smaller rooms of equal size. Allowing no room for aisles, the MINIMUM amount of partitioning that would be needed is _____ feet.

    A. 90   B. 100   C. 110   D. 140

24. Assume that two types of files have been ordered: 200 of type A and 100 of type B. When the files are delivered, the buyer discovers that 25% of each type is damaged. Of the remaining files, 20% of type A and 40% of type B are the wrong color.
    The total number of files that are the WRONG COLOR is

    A. 30   B. 40   C. 50   D. 60

25. In a unit of five inspectors, one inspector makes an average of 12 inspections a day, two inspectors make an average of 10 inspections a day, and two inspectors make an average of 9 inspections a day.
    If in a certain week one of the inspectors who makes an average of nine inspections a day is out of work on Monday and Tuesday because of illness and all the inspectors do no inspections for half a day on Wednesday because of a special meeting, the number of inspections this unit can be expected to make in that week is MOST NEARLY

    A. 215   B. 225   C. 230   D. 250

KEY (CORRECT ANSWERS)

1. B
2. C
3. D
4. D
5. D

6. C
7. B
8. B
9. A
10. D

11. A
12. C
13. C
14. C
15. B

16. B
17. A
18. A
19. B
20. B

21. C
22. D
23. B
24. D
25. A

SOLUTIONS TO PROBLEMS

1. Since the number of weekly inspections ranged from 20 to 40, this implies that the average weekly number of inspections never fell below 20 (choice B).

2. $591 \div .194 \approx 3046$, closest to 3000 students

3. $(591-268) \div 268 = 120\%$

4. Total processing cost = $(268)(\$28)+(1688)(\$21) = \$42,952$, closest to $40,000. [Note: Since 268 represents 13.7%, total freshman population = $268 \div .137 \approx 1956$. Then, $1956 - 268 = 1688$]

5. Let x = staff size in 2004-2005. Then, .80x = staff size in 2005-2006. Since the 2005-2006 staff produced 20% more work, this is represented by 1.20. However, to measure the productivity per staff member, the factor $1/.80 = 1.25$ must also be used to equate the 2 staffs. Then, $(1.20)(1.25) = 1.50$. Thus, the 2005-2006 staff produced 50% more work than the 2004-2005 staff.

6. The respective percent increases are $\approx 20\%, 17\%, 39\%, 29\%$. The largest would be, over the previous fiscal year, for the current fiscal year 2005-2006.

7. $\dfrac{P}{c}$ = number of buses needed per hour. If t = time (in hrs.), then $U_t = tP/c$

8. $a = (2)(9) = 18$ for 1 stop. Then, $288 \div 18 = 16$ stops

9. $560 \div .35 = 1600$ grand larcenies

10. $456 \div .226 = 2018$; $560 \div .35 = 1600$. Then, $(1600-2018) \div 2018 = -20\%$, or a 20% decrease

11. $(\dfrac{1}{6})(560) = 93\dfrac{1}{3}$. Then, $93\dfrac{1}{3} \div 1600 = 5.8\%$

12. There are 5000 brake jobs and 3000 front-end jobs in one year.
    $5000 \div 4 = 1250$ days, and $1250 \div 240 \approx 5.2$. Also, $3000 \div 3 = 1000$ days, and $1000 \div 240 \approx 4.2$. Total number of workers needed $\approx 5.2 + 4.2 \approx 10$

13. $(.94)(1.05)(1.10) = 1.0857$, which represents an overall increase by about 8.6%

14. Average annual % change = $(1+TC)^{\frac{1}{3}} - 1 = (1.0857)^{\frac{1}{3}} - 1 \approx 2.8\%$

15. $357 \div .06 = 5950$

16. In 2003, $(h)(1-\frac{k}{100})$ pieces cost $(x)(1+\frac{g}{100})$ dollars. To calculate the cost for 1 piece (average cost), find the value of $[(x)(1+\frac{G}{100})] \div [(n)(1-\frac{K}{100})] = [(x)(100+g)/100]$.

    $[100/\{n(100-k)\}] = [x(100+g)]/[n(100-k)]$

17.

	#	Deductions Up To 50,000	
40,000	6	2000 3000	40,000-3,000-2,000 = 35,000 x 6
80,000	10	2000 2000	80,000-2,000-2,000 = 76,000 x 10
20,000	2	2000	= 118000 x 2

   35,000 x 6 = 210,000 = 210
   76,000 x 10 = 760,000 = 760
   118,000 x 2 = 236,000 = 236
                                         1206

   $1206 \div 18 = 67$

18. 2002 Deductions

40,000	2	2000	3000	35,000 x 2 =	70,000
80,000	11	2000	2000	76,000 x 11 =	836,000
120,000	5	2000		118,000 x 5 =	590,000
					1,496,000

   1,496,000 / 18 = 83,111
   83,111 - 67,000 = 16,111 = most nearly 16 (in thousands)

19. We are actually looking for the number of different groups of different sizes involving S. This reduces to $_4C_1 + {_4C_2} + {_4C_2} + {_4C_4} = 4+6+4+1 = 15$. The notation nCr means combinations of n things taken R at a time $= [(n)(n-l)(n-2)(...)(n-R+l)] / [(R)(R-1)(...)(1)]$. The 15 groups are: SA, SB, SC, SD, SAB, SAC, SAD, SBC, SBD, SCD, SABC, SABD, SACD, SBCD, SABCD.

20. Let x = total premiums. Then, $\frac{.93}{100} = \frac{X}{8,765,000}$ Solving, x = $81,515

21. The balance, raised from property taxes, = $3,240,000,000 - $1,100,000,000 - $121,600,000 = $2,018,400,000. Now, (.60)($42,500,000,000) = $25,500,000. The tax rate per $100 of assessed value = ($2,018,400,000)($100)/$25,500,000,000 = $7.90

22. A dozen costs $(\$12.90)(\frac{12}{3}) = \$51.60$

23. $(40)(20) \div 8 = 100$ ft.

24. Total number of wrong-color files = $(200)(.75)(.20)+(100)(.75)(.40) = 60$

25. Weekly number of inspections = $(12 \times 5) + (10 \times 5) + (10 \times 5) + (9 \times 5) + (9 \times 5) = 250$
    Subtract: 9 Monday, 9 Tuesday, 25 Wednesday
    Total: $250 - 9 - 9 - 25 = 207$
    Closest entry is choice A

INTERPRETING STATISTICAL DATA GRAPHS, CHARTS AND TABLES
EXAMINATION SECTION
TEST 1

DIRECTIONS: Each question or incomplete statement is followed by several suggested answers or completions. Select the one that BEST answers the question or completes the statement. *PRINT THE LETTER OF THE CORRECT ANSWER IN THE SPACE AT THE RIGHT.*

Questions 1-3.

DIRECTIONS: Questions 1 through 3 are to be answered SOLELY on the basis of the following table.

QUARTERLY SALES REPORTED BY MAJOR INDUSTRY GROUPS

DECEMBER 2011 - FEBRUARY 2013
Reported Sales, Taxable & Non-Taxable
(In Millions)

Industry Groups	12/11-2/12	3/12-5/12	6/12-8/12	9/12-11/12	12/12-2/13
Retailers	2,802	2,711	2,475	2,793	2,974
Wholesalers	2,404	2,237	2,269	2,485	2,512
Manufacturers	3,016	2,888	3,001	3,518	3,293
Services	1,034	1,065	984	1,132	1,092

1. The trend in total reported sales may be described as

    A. downward
    B. downward and upward
    C. horizontal
    D. upward

1._____

2. The two industry groups that reveal a similar seasonal pattern for the period December 2011 through November 2012 are

    A. retailers and manufacturers
    B. retailers and wholesalers
    C. wholesalers and manufacturers
    D. wholesalers and service

2._____

3. Reported sales were at a MINIMUM between

    A. December 2011 and February 2012
    B. March 2012 and May 2012
    C. June 2012 and August 2012
    D. September 2012 and November 2012

3._____

TEST 2

DIRECTIONS: Each question or incomplete statement is followed by several suggested answers or completions. Select the one that BEST answers the question or completes the statement. *PRINT THE LETTER OF THE CORRECT ANSWER IN THE SPACE AT THE RIGHT.*

Questions 1-4.

DIRECTIONS: Questions 1 through 4 are to be answered SOLELY on the basis of the following information.

The income elasticity of demand for selected items of consumer demand in the United States are:

Item	Elasticity
Airline Travel	5.66
Alcohol	.62
Dentist Fees	1.00
Electric Utilities	3.00
Gasoline	1.29
Intercity Bus	1.89
Local Bus	1.41
Restaurant Meals	.75

1. The demand for the item listed below that would be MOST adversely affected by a decrease in income is

    A. alcohol
    B. electric utilities
    C. gasoline
    D. restaurant meals

2. The item whose relative change in demand would be the same as the relative change in income would be

    A. dentist fees
    B. gasoline
    C. restaurant meals
    D. none of the above

3. If income increases by 12 percent, the demand for restaurant meals may be expected to increase by

    A. 9 percent
    B. 12 percent
    C. 16 percent
    D. none of the above

4. On the basis of the above information, the item whose demand would be MOST adversely affected by an increase in the sales tax from 7 percent to 8 percent to be passed on to the consumer in the form of higher prices

    A. would be airline travel
    B. would be alcohol
    C. would be gasoline
    D. cannot be determined

1._
2._
3._
4._

TEST 3

DIRECTIONS: Each question or incomplete statement is followed by several suggested answers or completions. Select the one that BEST answers the question or completes the statement. *PRINT THE LETTER OF THE CORRECT ANSWER IN THE SPACE AT THE RIGHT.*

Questions 1-3.

DIRECTIONS: Questions 1 through 3 are to be answered SOLELY on the basis of the following graphs depicting various relationships in a single retail store.

GRAPH I
RELATIONSHIP BETWEEN NUMBER OF CUSTOMERS STORE AND TIME OF DAY

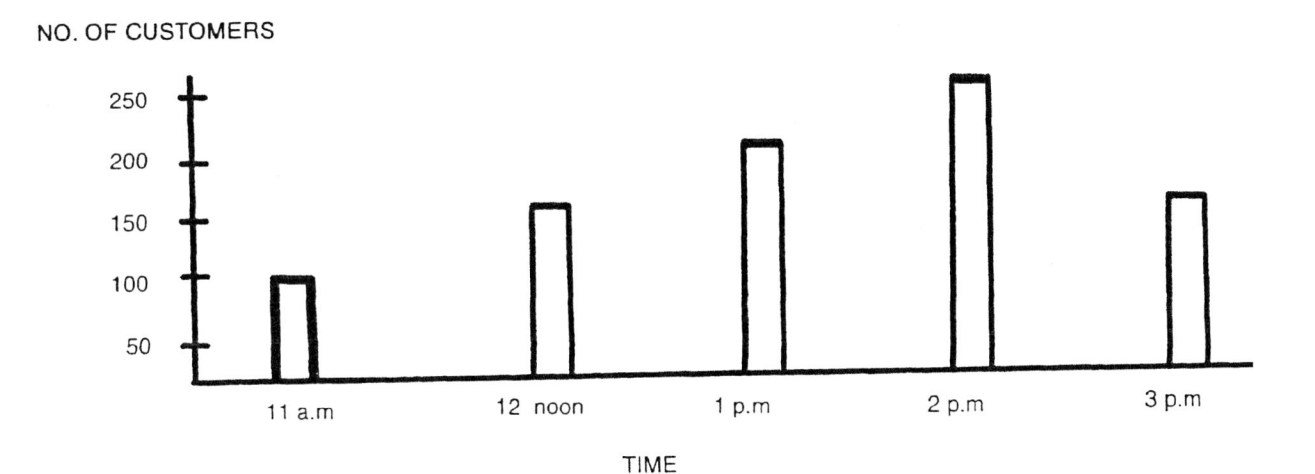

NO. OF CUSTOMERS

[Bar graph showing customers by time: 11 a.m ≈ 100, 12 noon ≈ 165, 1 p.m ≈ 215, 2 p.m ≈ 260, 3 p.m ≈ 175]

TIME

GRAPH II
RELATIONSHIP BETWEEN NUMBER OF CHECK-OUT LANES AVAILABLE IN STORE AND WAIT TIME FOR CHECK-OUT

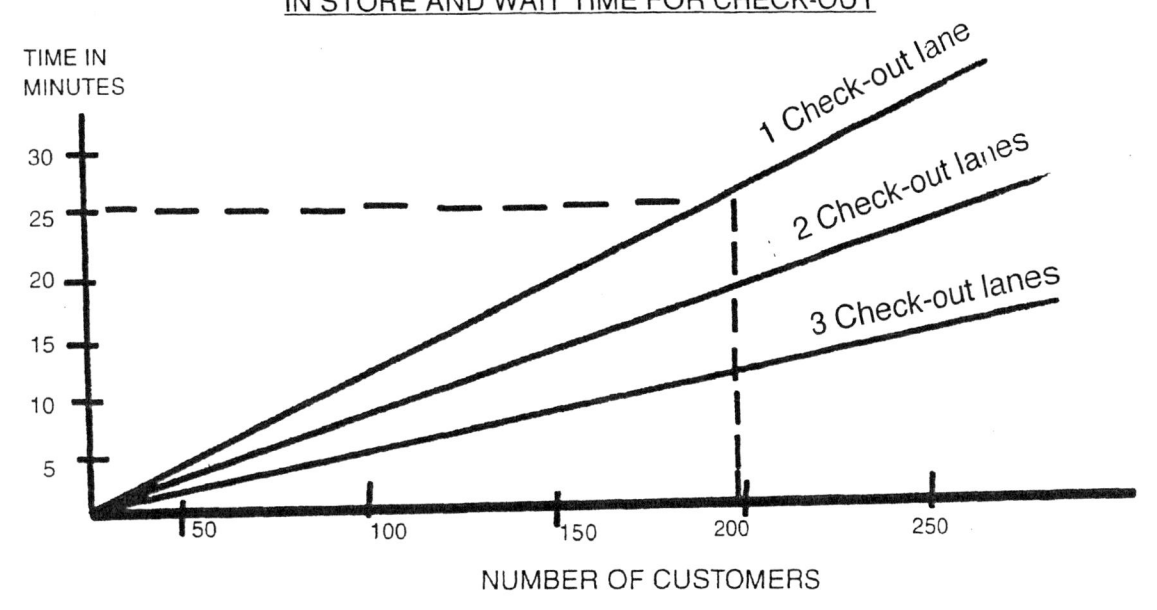

TIME IN MINUTES

[Line graph with three lines: 1 Check-out lane, 2 Check-out lanes, 3 Check-out lanes, plotted against NUMBER OF CUSTOMERS]

NUMBER OF CUSTOMERS

Note the dotted lines in Graph II. They demonstrate that, if there are 200 people in the store and only 1 check-out lane is open, the wait time will be 25 minutes.

1. At what time would a person be most likely NOT to have to wait more than 15 minutes if only one check-out lane is open?

   A. 11 A.M.   B. 12 Noon   C. 1 P.M.   D. 3 P.M.

2. At what time of day would a person have to wait the LONGEST to check out if 3 check-out lanes are available?

   A. 11 A.M.   B. 12 Noon   C. 1 P.M.   D. 2 P.M.

3. The difference in wait times between 1 and 3 check-out lanes at 3 P.M. is MOST NEARLY

   A. 5   B. 10   C. 15   D. 20

TEST 4

DIRECTIONS: Each question or incomplete statement is followed by several suggested answers or completions. Select the one that BEST answers the question or completes the statement. *PRINT THE LETTER OF THE CORRECT ANSWER IN THE SPACE AT THE RIGHT.*

Questions 1-4.

DIRECTIONS: Questions 1 through 4 are to be answered SOLELY on the basis of the graph below.

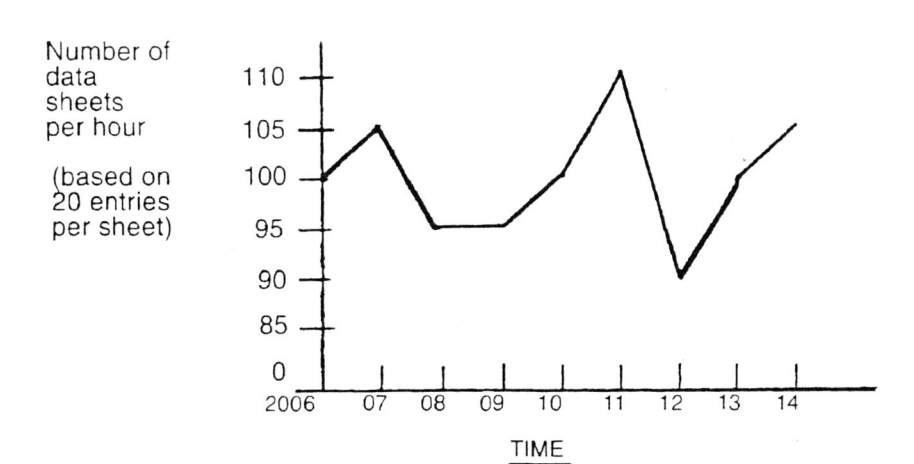

1. Of the following, during what four-year period did the average output of computer operators fall BELOW 100 sheets per hour?

   A. 2007-10   B. 2008-11   C. 2010-13   D. 2011-14

2. The average percentage change in output over the previous year's output for the years 2009 to 2012 is MOST NEARLY

   A. 2   B. 0   C. -5   D. -7

3. The difference between the actual output for 2002 and the projected figure based upon the average increase from 2006-2011 is MOST NEARLY

   A. 18   B. 20   C. 22   D. 24

4. Assume that after constructing the above graph you, an analyst, discovered that the average number of entries per sheet in 2012 was 25 (instead of 20) because of the complex nature of the work performed during that period.
The average output in cards per hour for the period 2010-13, expressed in terms of 20 items per sheet, would then be MOST NEARLY

   A. 95   B. 100   C. 105   D. 110

TEST 5

DIRECTIONS: Each question or incomplete statement is followed by several suggested answers or completions. Select the one that BEST answers the question or completes the statement. *PRINT THE LETTER OF THE CORRECT ANSWER IN THE SPACE AT THE RIGHT.*

Questions 1-3.

DIRECTIONS: Questions 1 through 3 are to be answered on the basis of the following data assembled for a cost-benefit analysis.

	Cost	Benefit
No program	0	0
Alternative W	$ 3,000	$ 6,000
Alternative X	$10,000	$17,000
Alternative Y	$17,000	$25,000
Alternative Z	$30,000	$32,000

1. From the point of view of selecting the alternative with the best cost benefit ratio, the BEST alternative is Alternative

    A. W   B. X   C. Y   D. Z

2. From the point of view of selecting the alternative with the best measure of net benefit, the BEST alternative is Alternative

    A. W   B. X   C. Y   D. Z

3. From the point of view of pushing public expenditure to the point where marginal benefit equals or exceeds marginal cost, the BEST alternative is Alternative

    A. W   B. X   C. Y   D. Z

TEST 6

DIRECTIONS: Each question or incomplete statement is followed by several suggested answers or completions. Select the one that BEST answers the question or completes the statement. *PRINT THE LETTER OF THE CORRECT ANSWER IN THE SPACE AT THE RIGHT.*

Questions 1-3.

DIRECTIONS: Questions 1 through 3 are to be answered SOLELY on the basis of the following data.

A series of cost-benefit studies of various alternative health programs yields the following results:

Program	Benefit	Cost
K	30	15
L	60	60
M	300	150
N	600	500

In answering Questions 1 and 2, assume that all programs can be increased or decreased in scale without affecting their individual benefit-to-cost ratios.

1. The benefit-to-cost ratio of Program M is

    A. 10:1   B. 5:1   C. 2:1   D. 1:2

2. The budget ceiling for one or more of the programs included in the study is set at 75 units.
   It may MOST logically be concluded that

    A. Programs K and L should be chosen to fit within the budget ceiling
    B. Program K would be the most desirable one that could be afforded
    C. Program M should be chosen rather than Program K
    D. the choice should be between Programs M and K

3. If no assumptions can be made regarding the effects of change of scale, the MOST logical conclusion, on the basis of the data available, is that

    A. more data are needed for a budget choice of program
    B. Program K is the most preferable because of its low cost and good benefit-to-cost ratio
    C. Program M is the most preferable because of its high benefits and good benefit-to-cost ratio
    D. there is no difference between Programs K and M, and either can be chosen for any purpose

TEST 7

DIRECTIONS: Each question or incomplete statement is followed by several suggested answers or completions. Select the one that BEST answers the question or completes the statement. *PRINT THE LETTER OF THE CORRECT ANSWER IN THE SPACE AT THE RIGHT.*

Questions 1-6.

DIRECTIONS: Questions 1 through 6 are to be answered SOLELY on the basis of the information contained in the charts below which relate to the budget allocations of City X, a small suburban community. The charts depict the annual budget allocations by Department and by expenditures over a five-year period.

CITY X BUDGET IN MILLIONS OF DOLLARS
TABLE I. Budget Allocations By Department

Department	2007	2008	2009	2010	2011
Public Safety	30	45	50	40	50
Health and Welfare	50	75	90	60	70
Engineering	5	8	10	5	8
Human Resources	10	12	20	10	22
Conservation & Environment	10	15	20	20	15
Education & Development	15	25	35	15	15
TOTAL BUDGET	120	180	225	150	180

TABLE II. Budget Allocations by Expenditures

Category	2007	2008	2009	2010	2011
Raw Materials & Machinery	36	63	68	30	98
Capital Outlay	12	27	56	15	18
Personal Services	72	90	101	105	64
TOTAL BUDGET	120	180	225	150	180

1. The year in which the SMALLEST percentage of the total annual budget was allocated to the Department of Education and Development is

    A. 2007　　B. 2008　　C. 2010　　D. 2011

2. Assume that in 2010 the Department of Conservation and Environment divided its annual budget into the three categories of expenditures and in exactly the same proportion as the budget shown in Table II for the year 2010. The amount allocated for capital outlay in the Department of Conservation and Environment's 2010 budget was MOST NEARLY _____ million.

    A. $2　　B. $4　　C. $6　　D. $10

3. From the year 2008 to the year 2010, the sum of the annual budgets for the Departments of Public Safety and Engineering showed an overall _____ million.

   A. decline; $8
   B. increase; $7
   C. decline; $15
   D. increase; $22

3._____

4. The LARGEST dollar increase in departmental budget allocations from one year to the next was in _____ from _____.

   A. Public Safety; 2007 to 2008
   B. Health and Welfare; 2007 to 2008
   C. Education and Development; 2009 to 2010
   D. Human Resources; 2009 to 2010

4._____

5. During the five-year period, the annual budget of the Department of Human Resources was GREATER than the annual budget for the Department of Conservation and Environment in _____ of the years.

   A. none   B. one   C. two   D. three

5._____

6. If the total City X budget increases at the same rate from 2011 to 2012 as it did from 2010 to 2011, the total City X budget for 2012 will be MOST NEARLY _____ million.

   A. $180   B. $200   C. $210   D. $215

6._____

TEST 8

DIRECTIONS: Each question or incomplete statement is followed by several suggested answers or completions. Select the one that BEST answers the question or completes the statement. *PRINT THE LETTER OF THE CORRECT ANSWER IN THE SPACE AT THE RIGHT.*

Questions 1-3.

DIRECTIONS: Questions 1 through 3 are to be answered SOLELY on the basis of the following information.

Assume that in order to encourage Program A, the State and Federal governments have agreed to make the following reimbursements for money spent on Program A, provided the unreimbursed balance is paid from City funds.

During Fiscal Year 2011-2012 - For the first $2 million expended, 50% Federal reimbursement and 30% State reimbursement; for the next $3 million, 40% Federal reimbursement and 20% State reimbursement; for the next $5 million, 20% Federal reimbursement and 10% State reimbursement. Above $10 million expended, no Federal or State reimbursement.

During Fiscal Year 2012-2013 - For the first $1 million expended, 30% Federal reimbursement and 20% State reimbursement; for the next $4 million, 15% Federal reimbursement and 10% State reimbursement. Above $5 million expended, no Federal or State reimbursement.

1. Assume that the Program A expenditures are such that the State reimbursement for Fiscal Year 2011-2012 will be $1 million.
   Then, the Federal reimbursement for Fiscal Year 2011-2012 will be

   A. $1,600,000 B. $1,800,000
   C. $2,000,000 D. $2,600,000

2. Assume that $8 million were to be spent on Program A in Fiscal Year 2012-2013.
   The TOTAL amount of unreimbursed City funds required would be

   A. $3,500,000 B. $4,500,000
   C. $5,500,000 D. $6,500,000

3. Assume that the City desires to have a combined total of $6 million spent in Program A during both the Fiscal Year 2011-2012 and the Fiscal Year 2012-2013.
   Of the following expenditure combinations, the one which results in the GREATEST reimbursement of City funds is _____ in Fiscal Year 2011-2012 and _____ in Fiscal Year 2012-2013.

   A. $5 million; $1 million B. $4 million; $2 million
   C. $3 million; $3 million D. $2 million; $4 million

KEY (CORRECT ANSWERS)

TEST 1	TEST 2	TEST 3	TEST 4
1. D	1. B	1. A	1. A
2. C	2. A	2. D	2. B
3. C	3. A	3. B	3. C
	4. D		4. C

TEST 5	TEST 6	TEST 7	TEST 8
1. A	1. C	1. D	1. B
2. C	2. D	2. A	2. D
3. C	3. A	3. A	3. A
		4. B	
		5. B	
		6. D	

READING COMPREHENSION
UNDERSTANDING AND INTERPRETING WRITTEN MATERIAL
EXAMINATION SECTION
TEST 1

DIRECTIONS: Each question or incomplete statement is followed by several suggested answers or completions. Select the one that BEST answers the question or completes the statement. *PRINT THE LETTER OF THE CORRECT ANSWER IN THE SPACE AT THE RIGHT.*

Questions 1-2.

DIRECTIONS: Questions 1 and 2 are to be answered SOLELY on the basis of the following passage.

The employees in a unit or division of a government agency may be referred to as a work group. Within a government agency which has existed for some time, the work groups will have evolved traditions of their own. The persons in these work groups acquire these traditions as part of the process of work adjustment within their groups. Usually, a work group in a large organization will contain *oldtimers*, *newcomers*, and *in-betweeners*. Like the supervisor of a group, who is not necessarily an oldtimer or the oldest member, oldtimers usually have great influence. They can recall events unknown to others and are a storehouse of information and advice about current problems in the light of past experience. They pass along the traditions of the group to the others who, in turn, become oldtimers themselves. Thus, the traditions of the group which have been honored and revered by long acceptance are continued.

1. According to the above passage, the traditions of a work group within a government agency are developed

    A. at the time the group is established
    B. over a considerable period of time
    C. in order to give recognition to oldtimers
    D. for the group before it is established

1.____

2. According to the above passage, the oldtimers within a work group

    A. are the means by which long accepted practices and customs are perpetuated
    B. would best be able to settle current problems that arise
    C. are honored because of the changes they have made in the traditions
    D. have demonstrated that they have learned to do their work well

2.____

Questions 3-4.

DIRECTIONS: Questions 3 and 4 are to be answered SOLELY on the basis of the following passage.

In public agencies, the success of a person assigned to perform first-line supervisory duties depends in large part upon the personal relations between him and his subordinate employees. The goal of supervising effort is something more than to obtain compliance with procedures established by some central office. The major objective is work accomplishment. In order for this goal to be attained, employees must want to attain it and must exercise initiative in their work. Only if employees are generally satisfied with the type of supervision which exists in an organization will they put forth their best efforts.

3. According to the above passage, in order for employees to try to do their work as well as they can, it is essential that

   A. they participate in determining their working conditions and rates of pay
   B. their supervisors support the employees' viewpoints in meetings with higher management
   C. they are content with the supervisory practices which are being used
   D. their supervisors make the changes in working procedures that the employees request

4. It can be inferred from the above passage that the goals of a unit in a public agency will not be reached unless the employees in the unit

   A. wish to reach them and are given the opportunity to make individual contributions to the work
   B. understand the relationship between the goals of the unit and goals of the agency
   C. have satisfactory personal relationships with employees of other units in the agency
   D. carefully follow the directions issued by higher authorities

Questions 5-9.

DIRECTIONS: Questions 5 through 9 are to be answered SOLELY on the basis of the following passage.

If an employee thinks he can save money, time, or material for the city or has an idea about how to do something better than it is being done, he shouldn't keep it to himself. He should send his ideas to the Employees' Suggestion Program, using the special form which is kept on hand in all departments. An employee may send in as many ideas as he wishes. To make sure that each idea is judged fairly, the name of the suggester is not made known until an award is made. The awards are certificates of merit or cash prizes ranging from $10 to $500.

5. According to the above passage, an employee who knows how to do a job in a better way should

   A. be sure it saves enough time to be worthwhile
   B. get paid the money he saves for the city
   C. keep it to himself to avoid being accused of causing a speed-up
   D. send his idea to the Employees' Suggestion Program

6. In order to send his idea to the Employees' Suggestion Program, an employee should 6.____

   A. ask the Department of Personnel for a special form
   B. get the special form in his own department
   C. mail the idea using Special Delivery
   D. send it on plain, white letter-size paper

7. An employee may send to the Employees' Suggestion Program 7.____

   A. as many ideas as he can think of
   B. no more than one idea each week
   C. no more than ten ideas in a month
   D. only one idea on each part of the job

8. The reason the name of an employee who makes a suggestion is not made known at first is to 8.____

   A. give the employee a larger award
   B. help the judges give more awards
   C. insure fairness in judging
   D. only one idea on each part of the job

9. An employee whose suggestion receives an award may be given a 9.____

   A. bonus once a year
   B. certificate for $10
   C. cash prize of up to $500
   D. salary increase of $500

Questions 10-12.

DIRECTIONS: Questions 10 through 12 are to be answered SOLELY on the basis of the following passage.

According to the rules of the Department of Personnel, the work of every permanent city employee is reviewed and rated by his supervisor at least once a year. The civil service rating system gives the employee and his supervisor a chance to talk about the progress made during the past year as well as about those parts of the job in which the employee needs to do better. In order to receive a pay increase each year, the employee must have a satisfactory service rating. Service ratings also count toward an employee's final mark on a promotion examination.

10. According to the above passage, a permanent city employee is rated AT LEAST once 10.____

    A. before his work is reviewed
    B. every six months
    C. yearly by his supervisor
    D. yearly by the Department of Personnel

11. According to the above passage, under the rating system the supervisor and the employee can discuss how 11.____

    A. much more work needs to be done next year
    B. the employee did his work last year

C. the work can be made easier next year
D. the work of the Department can be increased

12. According to the above passage, a permanent city employee will NOT receive a yearly pay increase

   A. if he received a pay increase the year before
   B. if he used his service rating for his mark on a promotion examination
   C. if his service rating is unsatisfactory
   D. unless he got some kind of a service rating

Questions 13-16.

DIRECTIONS: Questions 13 through 16 are to be answered SOLELY on the basis of the following passage.

It is an accepted fact that the rank and file employee can frequently advance worthwhile suggestions toward increasing efficiency. For this reason, an Employees' Suggestion System has been developed and put into operation. Suitable means have been provided at each departmental location for the confidential submission of suggestions. Numerous suggestions have been received thus far and, after study, about five percent of the ideas submitted are being translated into action. It is planned to set up, eventually, monetary awards for all worthwhile suggestions.

13. According to the above passage, a MAJOR reason why an Employees' Suggestion System was established is that

   A. an organized program of improvement is better than a haphazard one
   B. employees can often give good suggestions to increase efficiency
   C. once a fact is accepted, it is better to act on it than to do nothing
   D. the suggestions of rank and file employees were being neglected

14. According to the above passage, under the Employees' Suggestion System,

   A. a file of worthwhile suggestions will eventually be set up at each departmental location
   B. it is possible for employees to turn in suggestions without fellow employees knowing of it
   C. means have been provided for the regular and frequent collection of suggestions submitted
   D. provision has been made for the judging of worthwhile suggestions by an Employees' Suggestion Committee

15. According to the above passage, it is reasonable to assume that

   A. all suggestions must be turned in at a central office
   B. employees who make worthwhile suggestions will be promoted
   C. not all the prizes offered will be monetary ones
   D. prizes of money will be given for the best suggestions

16. According to the above passage, of the many suggestions made, 16.____

    A. all are first tested
    B. a small part are put into use
    C. most are very worthwhile
    D. samples are studied

Questions 17-20.

DIRECTIONS: Questions 17 through 20 are to be answered SOLELY on the basis of the following passage.

Employees may be granted leaves of absence without pay at the discretion of the Personnel Officer. Such a leave without pay shall begin on the first working day on which the employee does not report for duty and shall continue to the first day on which the employee returns to duty. The Personnel Division may vary the dates of the leave for the record so as to conform with payroll periods, but in no case shall an employee be off the payroll for a different number of calendar days than would have been the case if the actual dates mentioned above had been used. An employee who has vacation or overtime to his credit, which is available for normal use, may take time off immediately prior to beginning a leave of absence without pay, chargeable against all or part of such vacation or overtime.

17. According to the above passage, the Personnel Officer must 17.____

    A. decide if a leave of absence without pay should be granted
    B. require that a leave end on the last working day of a payroll period
    C. see to it that a leave of absence begins on the first working day of a pay period
    D. vary the dates of a leave of absence to conform with a payroll period

18. According to the above passage, the exact dates of a leave of absence without pay may be varied provided that the 18.____

    A. calendar days an employee is off the payroll equal the actual leave granted
    B. leave conforms to an even number of payroll periods
    C. leave when granted made provision for variance to simplify payroll records
    D. Personnel Officer approves the variation

19. According to the above passage, a leave of absence without pay must extend from the 19.____

    A. first day of a calendar period to the first day the employee resumes work
    B. first day of a payroll period to the last calendar day of the leave
    C. first working day missed to the first day on which the employee resumes work
    D. last day on which an employee works through the first day he returns to work

20. According to the above passage, an employee may take extra time off just before the start of a leave of absence without pay if 20.____

    A. he charges this extra time against his leave
    B. he has a favorable balance of vacation or overtime which has been frozen
    C. the vacation or overtime that he would normally use for a leave without pay has not been charged in this way before
    D. there is time to his credit which he may use

Question 21.

DIRECTIONS: Question 21 is to be answered SOLELY on the basis of the following passage.

In considering those things which are motivators and incentives to work, it might be just as erroneous not to give sufficient weight to money as an incentive as it is to give too much weight. It is not a problem of establishing a rank-order of importance, but one of knowing that motivation is a blend or mixture rather than a pure element. It is simple to say that cultural factors count more than financial considerations, but this leads only to the conclusion that our society is financial-oriented.

21. Based on the above passage, in our society, cultural and social motivations to work are

    A. things which cannot be avoided
    B. melded to financial incentives
    C. of less consideration than high pay
    D. not balanced equally with economic or financial considerations

Question 22.

DIRECTIONS: Question 22 is to be answered SOLELY on the basis of the following passage.

A general principle of training and learning with respect to people is that they learn more readily if they receive *feedback*. Essential to maintaining proper motivational levels is knowledge of results which indicate level of progress. Feedback also assists the learning process by identifying mistakes. If this kind of information were not given to the learner, then improper or inappropriate job performance may be instilled.

22. Based on the above passage, which of the following is MOST accurate?

    A. Learning will not take place without feedback.
    B. In the absence of feedback, improper or inappropriate job performance will be learned.
    C. To properly motivate a learner, the learner must have his progress made known to him.
    D. Trainees should be told exactly what to do if they are to learn properly.

Question 23.

DIRECTIONS: Question 23 is to be answered SOLELY on the basis of the following passage.

In a democracy, the obligation of public officials is twofold. They must not only do an efficient and satisfactory job of administration, but also they must persuade the public that it is an efficient and satisfactory job. It is a burden which, if properly assumed, will make democracy work and perpetuate reform government.

23. The above passage means that

    A. public officials should try to please everybody
    B. public opinion is instrumental in determining the policy of public officials

C. satisfactory performance of the job of administration will eliminate opposition to its work
D. frank and open procedure in a public agency will aid in maintaining progressive government

Question 24.

DIRECTIONS: Question 24 is to be answered SOLELY on the basis of the following passage.

Upon retirement for service, a member shall receive a retirement allowance which shall consist of an annuity which shall be the actuarial equivalent of his accumulated deductions at the time of his retirement and a pension, in addition to his annuity, which shall be equal to one service-fraction of his final compensation, multiplied by the number of years of service since he last became a member credited to him, and a pension which is the actuarial equivalent of the reserve-for-increased-take-home-pay to which he may then be entitled, if any.

24. According to the above passage, a retirement allowance shall consist of a(n)   24._____

  A. annuity, plus a pension, plus an actuarial equivalent
  B. annuity, plus a pension, plus reserve-for-increased-take-home-pay, if any
  C. annuity, plus reserve-for-increased-take-home-pay, if any, plus final compensation
  D. pension, plus reserve-for-increased-take-home-pay, if any, plus accumulated deductions

Question 25.

DIRECTIONS: Question 25 is to be answered SOLELY on the basis of the following passage.

Membership in the retirement system shall cease upon the occurrence of any one of the following conditions: when the time out of service of any member who has total service of less than 25 years, shall aggregate more than 5 years; when the time out of service of any member who has total service of 25 years or more, shall aggregate more than 10 years; when any member shall have withdrawn more than 50% of his accumulated deductions; or when any member shall have withdrawn the cash benefit provided by Section B3-35.0 of the Administrative Code.

25. According to the information in the above passage, membership in the retirement system   25._____
shall cease when an employee

  A. with 17 years of service has been on a leave of absence for 3 years
  B. withdraws 50% of his accumulated deductions
  C. with 28 years of service has been out of service for 10 years
  D. withdraws his cash benefits

KEY (CORRECT ANSWERS)

1.	B		11.	B
2.	A		12.	C
3.	C		13.	B
4.	A		14.	B
5.	D		15.	D
6.	B		16.	B
7.	A		17.	A
8.	C		18.	A
9.	B		19.	C
10.	C		20.	D

21. B
22. C
23. D
24. B
25. D

___

TEST 2

DIRECTIONS: Each question or incomplete statement is followed by several suggested answers or completions. Select the one that BEST answers the question or completes the statement. *PRINT THE LETTER OF THE CORRECT ANSWER IN THE SPACE AT THE RIGHT.*

Questions 1-6.

DIRECTIONS: Questions 1 through 6 are to be answered SOLELY on the basis of the following passage from an old office manual.

Since almost every office has some contact with data-processed records, a stenographer should have some understanding of the basic operations of data processing. Data processing systems now handle about one-third of all office paperwork. On punched cards, magnetic tape, or on other mediums, data are recorded before being fed into the computer for processing. A machine such as the keypunch is used to convert the data written on the source document into the coded symbols on punched cards or tapes. After data has been converted, it must be verified to guarantee absolute accuracy of conversion. In this manner, data becomes a permanent record which can be read by electronic computers that compare, store, compute, and otherwise process data at high speeds.

One key person in a computer installation is a programmer, the man or woman who puts business and scientific problems into special symbolic languages that can be read by the computer. Jobs done by the computer range all the way from payroll operations to chemical process control, but most computer applications are directed toward management data. About half of the programmers employed by business come to their positions with college degrees; the remaining half are promoted to their positions from within the organization on the basis of demonstrated ability without regard to education.

1. Of the following, the BEST title for the above passage is

   A. THE STENOGRAPHER AS DATA PROCESSOR
   B. THE RELATION OF KEYPUNCHING TO STENOGRAPHY
   C. UNDERSTANDING DATA PROCESSING
   D. PERMANENT OFFICE RECORDS

1._____

2. According to the above passage, a stenographer should understand the basic operations of data processing because

   A. almost every office today has contact with data processed by computer
   B. any office worker may be asked to verify the accuracy of data
   C. most offices are involved in the production of permanent records
   D. data may be converted into computer language by typing on a keypunch

2._____

3. According to the above passage, the data which the computer understands is MOST often expressed as

   A. a scientific programming language
   B. records or symbols punched on tape, cards, or other mediums
   C. records on cards
   D. records on tape

3._____

4. According to the above passage, computers are used MOST often to handle

 A. management data
 B. problems of higher education
 C. the control of chemical processes
 D. payroll operations

5. Computer programming is taught in many colleges and business schools. The above passage implies that programmers in industry

 A. must have professional training
 B. need professional training to advance
 C. must have at least a college education to do adequate programming tasks
 D. do not need college education to do programming work

6. According to the above passage, data to be processed by computer should be

 A. recent   B. basic
 C. complete   D. verified

Questions 7-10.

DIRECTIONS: Questions 7 through 10 are to be answered SOLELY on the basis of the following passage.

There is nothing that will take the place of good sense on the part of the stenographer. You may be perfect in transcribing exactly what the dictator says and your speed may be adequate, but without an understanding of the dictator's intent as well as his words, you are likely to be a mediocre secretary.

A serious error that is made when taking dictation is putting down something that does not make sense. Most people who dictate material would rather be asked to repeat and explain than to receive transcribed material which has errors due to inattention or doubt. Many dictators request that their grammar be corrected by their secretaries, but unless specifically asked to do so, secretaries should not do it without first checking with the dictator. Secretaries should be aware that, in some cases, dictators may use incorrect grammar or slang expressions to create a particular effect.

Some people dictate commas, periods, and paragraphs, while others expect the stenographer to know when, where, and how to punctuate. A well-trained secretary should be able to indicate the proper punctuation by listening to the pauses and tones of the dictator's voice.

A stenographer who has taken dictation from the same person for a period of time should be able to understand him under most conditions, By increasing her tact, alertness, and efficiency, a secretary can become more competent.

7. According to the above passage, which of the following statements concerning the dictation of punctuation is CORRECT?

 A. Dictator may use incorrect punctuation to create a desired style
 B. Dictator should indicate all punctuation
 C. Stenographer should know how to punctuate based on the pauses and tones of the dictator
 D. Stenographer should not type any punctuation if it has not been dictated to her

8. According to the above passage, how should secretaries handle grammatical errors in a dictation? Secretaries should 8._____

   A. *not correct* grammatical errors unless the dictator is aware that this is being done
   B. *correct* grammatical errors by having the dictator repeat the line with proper pauses
   C. *correct* grammatical errors if they have checked the correctness in a grammar book
   D. *correct* grammatical errors based on their own good sense

9. If a stenographer is confused about the method of spacing and indenting of a report which has just been dictated to her, she GENERALLY should 9._____

   A. do the best she can
   B. ask the dictator to explain what she should do
   C. try to improve her ability to understand dictated material
   D. accept the fact that her stenographic ability is not adequate

10. In the last line of the first paragraph, the word *mediocre* means MOST NEARLY 10._____

    A. superior
    C. disregarded
    B. respected
    D. second-rate

Questions 11-12.

DIRECTIONS: Questions 11 and 12 are to be answered SOLELY on the basis of the following passage.

   The number of legible carbon copies required to be produced determines the weight of the carbon paper to be used. When only one copy is made, heavy carbon paper is satisfactory. Most typists, however, use medium-weight carbon paper and find it serviceable for up to three or four copies. If five or more copies are to be made, it is wise to use light carbon paper. On the other hand, the finish of carbon paper to be used depends largely on the stroke of the typist and, in lesser degree, on the number of copies to be made and on whether the typewriter has pica or elite type. A soft-finish carbon paper should be used if the typist's touch is light or if a noiseless machine is used. It is desirable for the average typist to use medium-finish carbon paper for ordinary work, when only a few carbon copies are required. Elite type requires a harder carbon finish than pica type for the same number of copies.

11. According to the above passage, the lighter the carbon paper used, 11._____

    A. the softer the finish of the carbon paper will be
    B. the greater the number of legible carbon copies that can be made
    C. the greater the number of times the carbon paper can be used
    D. the lighter the typist's touch should be

12. According to the above passage, the MOST important factor which determines whether the finish of carbon paper to be used in typing should be hard, medium, or soft is 12._____

    A. the touch of the typist
    B. the number of carbon copies required
    C. whether the type in the typewriter is pica or elite
    D. whether a machine with pica type will produce the same number of carbon copies as a machine with elite type

Questions 13-16.

DIRECTIONS: Questions 13 through 16 are to be answered SOLELY on the basis of the following passage.

Modern office methods, geared to ever higher speeds and aimed at ever greater efficiency, are largely the result of the typewriter. The typewriter is a substitute for handwriting and, in the hands of a skilled typist, not only turns out letters and other documents at least three times faster than a penman can do the work, but turns out the greater volume more uniformly and legibly. With the use of carbon paper and onionskin paper, identical copies can be made at the same time.

The typewriter, besides its effect on the conduct of business and government, has had a very important effect on the position of women. The typewriter has done much to bring women into business and government, and today there are vastly more women than men typists. Many women have used the keys of the typewriter to climb the ladder to responsible managerial positions.

The typewriter, as its name implies, employs type to make an ink impression on paper. For many years, the manual typewriter was the standard machine used. Today, the electric typewriter is dominant, and completely automatic electronic typewriters are coming into wider use.

The mechanism of the office manual typewriter includes a set of keys arranged systematically in rows; a semicircular frame of type, connected to the keys by levers; the carriage, or paper carrier; a rubber roller, called a platen, against which the type strikes; and an inked ribbon which make the impression of the type character when the key strikes it.

13. The above passage mentions a number of good features of the combination of a skilled typist and a typewriter. Of the following, the feature which is NOT mentioned in the passage is

    A. speed
    B. reliability
    C. uniformity
    D. legibility

14. According to the above passage, a skilled typist can

    A. turn out at least five carbon copies of typed matter
    B. type at least three times faster than a penman can write
    C. type more than 80 words a minute
    D. readily move into a managerial position

15. According to the above passage, which of the following is NOT part of the mechanism of a manual typewriter?

    A. Carbon paper
    B. Platen
    C. Paper carrier
    D. Inked ribbon

16. According to the above passage, the typewriter has helped

    A. men more than women in business
    B. women in career advancement into management
    C. men and women equally, but women have taken better advantage of it
    D. more women than men, because men generally dislike routine typing work

Questions 17-21.

DIRECTIONS: Questions 17 through 21 are to be answered SOLELY on the basis of the following passage.

The recipient gains an impression of a typewritten letter before he begins to read the message. Factors which provide for a good first impression include margins and spacing that are visually pleasing, formal parts of the letter which are correctly placed according to the style of the letter, copy which is free of obvious erasures and over-strikes, and transcript that is even and clear. The problem for the typist is that of how to produce that first, positive impression of her work.

There are several general rules which a typist can follow when she wishes to prepare a properly spaced letter on a sheet of letterhead. Ordinarily, the width of a letter should not be less than four inches nor more than six inches. The side margins should also have a desirable relation to the bottom margin and the space between the letterhead and the body of the letter. Usually the most appealing arrangement is when the side margins are even and the bottom margin is slightly wider than the side margins. In some offices, however, standard line length is used for all business letters, and the secretary then varies the spacing between the date line and the inside address according to the length of the letter.

17. The BEST title for the above passage would be   17._____

    A. WRITING OFFICE LETTERS
    B. MAKING GOOD FIRST IMPRESSIONS
    C. JUDGING WELL-TYPED LETTERS
    D. GOOD PLACING AND SPACING FOR OFFICE LETTERS

18. According to the above passage, which of the following might be considered the way in   18._____
    which people very quickly judge the quality of work which has been typed? By

    A. measuring the margins to see if they are correct
    B. looking at the spacing and cleanliness of the typescript
    C. scanning the body of the letter for meaning
    D. reading the date line and address for errors

19. What, according to the above passage, would be definitely UNDESIRABLE as the average line length of a typed letter?   19._____

    A. 4"   B. 6"
    C. 5"   D. 7"

20. According to the above passage, when the line length is kept standard, the secretary   20._____

    A. does not have to vary the spacing at all since this also is standard
    B. adjusts the spacing between the date line and inside address for different lengths of letters
    C. uses the longest line as a guideline for spacing between the date line and inside address
    D. varies the number of spaces between the lines

21. According to the above passage, side margins are MOST pleasing when they

    A. are even and somewhat smaller than the bottom margin
    B. are slightly wider than the bottom margin
    C. vary with the length of the letter
    D. are figured independently from the letterhead and the body of the letter

Questions 22-25.

DIRECTIONS: Questions 22 through 25 are to be answered SOLELY on the basis of the following passage.

    Typed pages can reflect the simplicity of modern art in a machine age. Lightness and evenness can be achieved by proper layout and balance of typed lines and white space. Instead of solid, cramped masses of uneven, crowded typing, there should be a pleasing balance up and down as well as horizontal.

    To have real balance, your page must have a center. The eyes see the center of the sheet slightly above the real center. This is the way both you and the reader see it. Try imagining a line down the center of the page that divides the paper in equal halves. On either side of your paper, white space and blocks of typing need to be similar in size and shape. Although left and right margins should be equal, top and bottom margins need not be as exact. It looks better to hold a bottom border wider than a top margin, so that your typing rests upon a cushion of white space. To add interest to the appearance of the page, try making one paragraph between one-half and two-thirds the size of an adjacent paragraph.

    Thus, by taking full advantage of your typewriter, the pages that you type will not only be accurate but will also be attractive.

22. It can be inferred from the above passage that the basic importance of proper balancing on a typed page is that proper balancing

    A. makes a typed page a work of modern art
    B. provides exercise in proper positioning of a typewriter
    C. increases the amount of typed copy on the paper
    D. draws greater attention and interest to the page

23. A reader will tend to see the center of a typed page

    A. somewhat higher than the true center
    B. somewhat lower than the true center
    C. on either side of the true center
    D. about two-thirds of an inch above the true center

24. Which of the following suggestions is NOT given by the above passage?

    A. Bottom margins may be wider than top borders.
    B. Keep all paragraphs approximately the same size.
    C. Divide your page with an imaginary line down the middle.
    D. Side margins should be equalized.

25. Of the following, the BEST title for the above passage is 25._____
    A. INCREASING THE ACCURACY OF THE TYPED PAGE
    B. DETERMINATION OF MARGINS FOR TYPED COPY
    C. LAYOUT AND BALANCE OF THE TYPED PAGE
    D. HOW TO TAKE FULL ADVANTAGE OF THE TYPEWRITER

KEY (CORRECT ANSWERS)

1.	C	11.	B
2.	A	12.	A
3.	B	13.	C
4.	A	14.	B
5.	D	15.	A
6.	D	16.	B
7.	C	17.	D
8.	A	18.	B
9.	B	19.	D
10.	D	20.	B

21. A
22. D
23. A
24. B
25. C

TEST 3

DIRECTIONS: Each question or incomplete statement is followed by several suggested answers or completions. Select the one that BEST answers the question or completes the statement. *PRINT THE LETTER OF THE CORRECT ANSWER IN THE SPACE AT THE RIGHT.*

Questions 1-5.

DIRECTIONS: Questions 1 through 5 are to be answered SOLELY on the basis of the following passage.

    A written report is a communication of information from one person to another. It is an account of some matter especially investigated, however routine that matter may be. The ultimate basis of any good written report is facts, which become known through observation and verification. Good written reports may seem to be no more than general ideas and opinions. However, in such cases, the facts leading to these opinions were gathered, verified, and reported earlier, and the opinions are dependent upon these facts. Good style, proper form, and emphasis cannot make a good written report out of unreliable information and bad judgment; but on the other hand, solid investigation and brilliant thinking are not likely to become very useful until they are effectively communicated to others. If a person's work calls for written reports, then his work is often no better than his written reports.

1. Based on the information in the above passage, it can be concluded that opinions expressed in a report should be

    A. based on facts which are gathered and reported
    B. emphasized repeatedly when they result from a special investigation
    C. kept to a minimum
    D. separated from the body of the report

2. In the above passage, the one of the following which is mentioned as a way of establishing facts is

    A. authority   B. reporting
    C. communication   D. verification

3. According to the above passage, the characteristic shared by ALL written reports is that they are

    A. accounts of routine matters   B. transmissions of information
    C. reliable and logical   D. written in proper form

4. Which of the following conclusions can logically be drawn from the information given in the above passage?

    A. Brilliant thinking can make up for unreliable information in a report.
    B. One method of judging an individual's work is the quality of the written reports he is required to submit.
    C. Proper form and emphasis can make a good report out of unreliable information.
    D. Good written reports that seem to be no more than general ideas should be rewritten.

5. Which of the following suggested titles would be MOST appropriate for the above passage?   5.___

   A. GATHERING AND ORGANIZING FACTS
   B. TECHNIQUES OF OBSERVATION
   C. NATURE AND PURPOSE OF REPORTS
   D. REPORTS AND OPINIONS: DIFFERENCES AND SIMILARITIES

Questions 6-8.

DIRECTIONS: Questions 6 through 8 are to be answered SOLELY on the basis of the following passage.

The most important unit of the mimeograph machine is a perforated metal drum over which is stretched a cloth ink pad. A reservoir inside the drum contains the ink which flows through the perforations and saturates the ink pad. To operate the machine, the operator first removes from the machine the protective sheet, which keeps the ink from drying while the machine is not in use. He then hooks the stencil face down on the drum, draws the stencil smoothly over the drum, and fastens the stencil at the bottom. The speed with which the drum turns determines the blackness of the copies printed. Slow turning gives heavy, black copies; fast turning gives light, clear-cut reproductions. If reproductions are run on other than porous paper, slip-sheeting is necessary to prevent smearing. Often, the printed copy fails to drop readily as it comes from the machine. This may be due to static electricity. To remedy this difficulty, the operator fastens a strip of tinsel from side to side near the impression roller so that the printed copy just touches the soft stems of the tinsel as it is ejected from the machine, thus grounding the static electricity to the frame of the machine.

6. According to the above passage,   6.___

   A. turning the drum fast produces light copies
   B. stencils should be placed face up on the drum
   C. ink pads should be changed daily
   D. slip-sheeting is necessary when porous paper is being used

7. According to the above passage, when a mimeograph machine is not in use,   7.___

   A. the ink should be drained from the drum
   B. the ink pad should be removed
   C. the machine should be covered with a protective sheet
   D. the counter should be set at zero

8. According to the above passage, static electricity is grounded to the frame of the mimeograph machine by means of   8.___

   A. a slip-sheeting device
   B. a strip of tinsel
   C. an impression roller
   D. hooks located at the top of the drum

Questions 9-10.

DIRECTIONS: Questions 9 and 10 are to be answered SOLELY on the basis of the following passage.

The proofreading of material typed from copy is performed more accurately and more speedily when two persons perform this work as a team. The person who did not do the typing should read aloud the original copy while the person who did the typing should check the reading against the typed copy. The reader should speak very slowly and repeat the figures, using a different grouping of numbers when repeating the figures. For example, in reading 1967, the reader may say *one-nine-six-seven* on first reading the figure and *nineteen-sixty-seven* on repeating the figure. The reader should read all punctuation marks, taking nothing for granted. Since mistakes can occur anywhere, everything typed should be proofread. To avoid confusion, the proofreading team should use the standard proofreading marks, which are given in most dictionaries.

9. According to the above passage, the

    A. person who holds the typed copy is called the reader
    B. two members of a proofreading team should take turns in reading the typed copy aloud
    C. typed copy should be checked by the person who did the typing
    D. person who did not do the typing should read aloud from the typed copy

10. According to the above passage,

    A. it is unnecessary to read the period at the end of a sentence
    B. typographical errors should be noted on the original copy
    C. each person should develop his own set of proofreading marks
    D. figures should be read twice

Questions 11-16.

DIRECTIONS: Questions 11 through 16 are to be answered SOLELY on the basis of the above passage.

Basic to every office is the need for proper lighting. Inadequate lighting is a familiar cause of fatigue and serves to create a somewhat dismal atmosphere in the office. One requirement of proper lighting is that it be of an appropriate intensity. Intensity is measured in foot candles. According to the Illuminating Engineering Society of New York, for casual seeing tasks such as in reception rooms, inactive file rooms, and other service areas, it is recommended that the amount of light be 30 foot-candles. For ordinary seeing tasks such as reading, work in active file rooms, and in mailrooms, the recommended lighting is 100 foot-candles. For very difficult seeing tasks such as accounting, transcribing, and business machine use, the recommended lighting is 150 foot-candles.

Lighting intensity is only one requirement. Shadows and glare are to be avoided. For example, the larger the proportion of a ceiling filled with lighting units, the more glare-free and comfortable the lighting will be. Natural lighting from windows is not too dependable because on dark wintry days, windows yield little usable light, and on sunny summer afternoons, the glare from windows may be very distracting. Desks should not face the windows. Finally, the main lighting source ought to be overhead and to the left of the user,

11. According to the above passage, insufficient light in the office may cause 11.____

    A. glare   B. tiredness
    C. shadows   D. distraction

12. Based on the above passage, which of the following must be considered when planning 12.____
    lighting arrangements? The

    A. amount of natural light present
    B. amount of work to be done
    C. level of difficulty of work to be done
    D. type of activity to be carried out

13. It can be inferred from the above passage that a well-coordinated lighting scheme is 13.____
    LIKELY to result in

    A. greater employee productivity
    B. elimination of light reflection
    C. lower lighting cost
    D. more use of natural light

14. Of the following, the BEST title for the above passage is 14.____

    A. CHARACTERISTICS OF LIGHT
    B. LIGHT MEASUREMENT DEVICES
    C. FACTORS TO CONSIDER WHEN PLANNING LIGHTING SYSTEMS
    D. COMFORT VS. COST WHEN DEVISING LIGHTING ARRANGEMENTS

15. According to the above passage, a foot-candle is a measurement of the 15.____

    A. number of bulbs used
    B. strength of the light
    C. contrast between glare and shadow
    D. proportion of the ceiling filled with lighting units

16. According to the above passage, the number of foot-candles of light that would be 16.____
    needed to copy figures onto a payroll is _____ foot-candles.

    A. less than 30   B. 100
    C. 30   D. 150

Questions 17-23.

DIRECTIONS: Questions 17 through 23 are to be answered SOLELY on the basis of the following passage, which is the Fee Schedule of a hypothetical college.

FEE SCHEDULE

A. A candidate for any baccalaureate degree is not required to pay tuition fees for undergraduate courses until he exceeds 128 credits, Candidates exceeding 128 credits in undergraduate courses are charged at the rate of $100 a credit for each credit of undergraduate course work in excess of 128. Candidates for a baccalaureate degree who are taking graduate courses must pay the same fee as any other student taking graduate courses

B. Non-degree students and college graduates are charged tuition fees for courses, whether undergraduate or graduate, at the rate of $180 a credit. For such students, there is an additional charge of $150 for each class hour per week in excess of the number of course credits. For example, if a three-credit course meets five hours a week, there is an additional charge for the extra two hours. Graduate courses are shown with a (G) before the course number.

C. All students are required to pay the laboratory fees indicated after the number of credits given for that course.

D. All students must pay a $250 general fee each semester.

E. Candidates for a baccalaureate degree are charged a $150 medical insurance fee for each semester. All other students are charged a $100 medical insurance fee each semester.

17. Miss Burton is not a candidate for a degree. She registers for the following courses in the spring semester: Economics 12, 4 hours a week, 3 credits; History (G) 23, 4 hours a week, 3 credits; English 1, 2 hours a week, 2 credits. The TOTAL amount in fees that Miss Burton must pay is

    A. less than $2000
    B. at least $2000 but less than $2100
    C. at least $2100 but less than $2200
    D. $2200 or over

18. Miss Gray is not a candidate for a degree. She registers for the following courses in the fall semester: History 3, 3 hours a week, 3 credits; English 5, 3 hours a week, 2 credits; Physics 5, 6 hours a week, 3 credits, laboratory fee $60; Mathematics 7, 4 hours a week, 3 credits. The TOTAL amount in fees that Miss Gray must pay is

    A. less than $3150
    B. at least $3150 but less than $3250
    C. at least $3250 but less than $3350
    D. $3350 or over

19. Mr. Wall is a candidate for the Bachelor of Arts degree and has completed 126 credits. He registers for the following courses in the spring semester, his final semester at college: French 4, 3 hours a week, 3 credits; Physics (G) 15, 6 hours a week, 3 credits, laboratory fee $80; History (G) 33, 4 hours a week, 3 credits. The TOTAL amount in fees that this candidate must pay is

    A. less than $2100
    B. at least $2100 but less than $2300
    C. at least $2300 but less than $2500
    D. $2500

20. Mr. Tindall, a candidate for the B.A. degree, has completed 122 credits of undergraduate courses. He registers for the following courses in his final semester: English 31, 3 hours a week, 3 credits; Philosophy 12, 4 hours a week, 4 credits; Anthropology 15, 3 hours a week, 3 credits; Economics (G) 68, 3 hours a week, 3 credits. The TOTAL amount in fees that Mr. Tindall must pay in his final semester is

    A. less than $1200
    B. at least $1200 but less than $1400
    C. at least $1400 but less than $1600
    D. $1600

21. Mr. Cantrell, who was graduated from the college a year ago, registers for graduate courses in the fall semester. Each course for which he registers carries the same number of credits as the number of hours a week it meets.
If he pays a total of $1530; including a $100 laboratory fee, the number of credits for which he is registered is

   A. 4   B. 5   C. 6   D. 7

21.____

22. Miss Jayson, who is not a candidate for a degree, has, registered for several courses including a lecture course in History. She withdraws from the course in History for which she had paid the required course fee of $690. The number of hours that this course is scheduled to meet is

   A. 4   B. 5   C. 2   D. 3

22.____

23. Mr. Van Arsdale, a graduate of a college is Iowa, registers for the following courses in one semester: Chemistry 35, 5 hours a week, 3 credits; Biology 13, 4 hours a week, 3 credits, laboratory fee $150; Mathematics (G) 179, 3 hours a week, 3 credits.
The TOTAL amount in fees that Mr. Van Arsdale must pay is

   A. less than $2400
   B. at least $2400 but less than $2500
   C. at least $2500 but less than $2600
   D. at least $2600 or over

23.____

Questions 24-25.

DIRECTIONS: Questions 24 and 25 are to be answered SOLELY on the basis of the following passage.

A duplex envelope is an envelope composed of two sections securely fastened together so that they become one mailing piece. This type of envelope makes it possible for a first class letter to be delivered simultaneously with third or fourth class matter and yet not require payment of the much higher first class postage rate on the entire mailing. First class postage is paid only on the letter which goes in the small compartment, third or fourth class postage being paid on the contents of the larger compartment. The larger compartment generally has an ungummed flap or clasp for sealing. The first class or smaller compartment has a gummed flap for sealing. Postal regulations require that the exact amount of postage applicable to each compartment be separately attached to it.

24. On the basis of the above passage, it is MOST accurate to state that

   A. the smaller compartment is placed inside the larger compartment before mailing
   B. the two compartments may be detached and mailed separately
   C. two classes of mailing matter may be mailed as a unit at two different postage rates
   D. the more expensive postage rate is paid on the matter in the larger compartment

24.____

25. When a duplex envelope is used, the 25.___
    A. first class compartment may be sealed with a clasp
    B. correct amount of postage must be placed on each compartment
    C. compartment containing third or fourth class mail requires a gummed flap for sealing
    D. full amount of postage for both compartments may be placed on the larger compartment

KEY (CORRECT ANSWERS)

1.	A	11.	C
2.	D	12.	D
3.	B	13.	A
4.	B	14.	C
5.	C	15.	B
6.	A	16.	D
7.	C	17.	B
8.	B	18.	A
9.	C	19.	B
10.	D	20.	B

21. C
22. A
23. C
24. C
25. B

PREPARING WRITTEN MATERIAL

PARAGRAPH REARRANGEMENT
COMMENTARY

The sentences which follow are in scrambled order. You are to rearrange them in proper order and indicate the letter choice containing the correct answer at the space at the right.

Each group of sentences in this section is actually a paragraph presented in scrambled order. Each sentence in the group has a place in that paragraph; no sentence is to be left out. You are to read each group of sentences and decide upon the best order in which to put the sentences so as to form as well-organized paragraph.

The questions in this section measure the ability to solve a problem when all the facts relevant to its solution are not given.

More specifically, certain positions of responsibility and authority require the employee to discover connections between events sometimes, apparently, unrelated. In order to do this, the employee will find it necessary to correctly infer that unspecified events have probably occurred or are likely to occur. This ability becomes especially important when action must be taken on incomplete information.

Accordingly, these questions require competitors to choose among several suggested alternatives, each of which presents a different sequential arrangement of the events. Competitors must choose the MOST logical of the suggested sequences.

In order to do so, they may be required to draw on general knowledge to infer missing concepts or events that are essential to sequencing the given events. Competitors should be careful to infer only what is essential to the sequence. The plausibility of the wrong alternatives will always require the inclusion of unlikely events or of additional chains of events which are NOT essential to sequencing the given events.

It's very important to remember that you are looking for the best of the four possible choices, and that the best choice of all may not even be one of the answers you're given to choose from.

There is no one right way to these problems. Many people have found it helpful to first write out the order of the sentences, as they would have arranged them, on their scrap paper before looking at the possible answers. If their optimum answer is there, this can save them some time. If it isn't, this method can still give insight into solving the problem. Others find it most helpful to just go through each of the possible choices, contrasting each as they go along. You should use whatever method feels comfortable, and works, for you.

While most of these types of questions are not that difficult, we've added a higher percentage of the difficult type, just to give you more practice. Usually there are only one or two questions on this section that contain such subtle distinctions that you're unable to answer confidently, and you then may find yourself stuck deciding between two possible choices, neither of which you're sure about.

EXAMINATION SECTION
TEST 1

DIRECTIONS: The sentences that follow are in scrambled order. You are to rearrange them in proper order and indicate the letter choice containing the correct answer. *PRINT THE LETTER OF THE CORRECT ANSWER IN THE SPACE AT THE RIGHT.*

1. Below are four statements labeled W., X., Y., and Z. 1.____
   W. He was a strict and fanatic drillmaster.
   X. The word is always used in a derogatory sense and generally shows resentment and anger on the part of the user.
   Y. It is from the name of this Frenchman that we derive our English word, martinet.
   Z. Jean Martinet was the Inspector-General of Infantry during the reign of King Louis XIV.

   The *PROPER* order in which these sentences should be placed in a paragraph is:

   A. X, Z, W, Y   B. X, Z, Y, W   C. Z, W, Y, X   D. Z, Y, W, X

2. In the following paragraph, the sentences which are numbered, have been jumbled. 2.____
   1. Since then it has undergone changes.
   2. It was incorporated in 1955 under the laws of the State of New York.
   3. Its primary purpose, a cleaner city, has, however, remained the same.
   4. The Citizens Committee works in cooperation with the Mayor's Inter-departmental Committee for a Clean City.

   The order in which these sentences should be arranged to form a well-organized paragraph is:

   A. 2, 4, 1, 3   B. 3, 4, 1, 2   C. 4, 2, 1, 3   D. 4, 3, 2, 1

Questions 3-5.

DIRECTIONS: The sentences listed below are part of a meaningful paragraph but they are not given in their proper order. You are to decide what would be the *best order* in which to put the sentences so as to form a well-organized paragraph. Each sentence has a place in the paragraph; there are no extra sentences. You are then to answer questions 3 to 5 inclusive on the basis of your rearrangements of these secrambled sentences into a properly organized paragraph.

In 1887 some insurance companies organized an Inspection Department to advise their clients on all phases of fire prevention and protection. Probably this has been due to the smaller annual fire losses in Great Britain than in the United States. It tests various fire prevention devices and appliances and determines manufacturing hazards and their safeguards. Fire research began earlier in the United States and is more advanced than in Great Britain. Later they established a laboratory specializing in electrical, mechanical, hydraulic, and chemical fields.

3. When the five sentences are arranged in proper order, the paragraph starts with the sentence which begins   3.___

    A. "In 1887..."   B. "Probably this ..."   C. "It tests ..."
    D. "Fire research ..."   E. "Later they ..."

4. In the last sentence listed above, "they" refers to   4.___

    A. insurance companies
    B. the United States and Great Britain
    C. the Inspection Department
    D. clients
    E. technicians

5. When the above paragraph is properly arranged, it ends with the words   5.___

    A. "... and protection."   B. "... the United States."
    C. "... their safeguards."   D. "... in Great Britain."
    E. "... chemical fields."

KEY (CORRECT ANSWERS)

1. C
2. C
3. D
4. A
5. C

TEST 2

DIRECTIONS: In each of the questions numbered 1 through 5, several sentences are given. For each question, choose as your answer the group of numbers that represents the *most logical* order of these sentences if they were arranged in paragraph form. *PRINT THE LETTER OF THE CORRECT ANSWER IN THE SPACE AT THE RIGHT.*

1. 1. It is established when one shows that the landlord has prevented the tenant's enjoyment of his interest in the property leased.
    2. Constructive eviction is the result of a breach of the covenant of quiet enjoyment implied in all leases.
    3. In some parts of the United States, it is not complete until the tenant vacates within a reasonable time.
    4. Generally, the acts must be of such serious and permanent character as to deny the tenant the enjoyment of his possessing rights.
    5. In this event, upon abandonment of the premises, the tenant's liability for that ceases.

    The CORRECT answer is:

    A. 2, 1, 4, 3, 5   B. 5, 2, 3, 1, 4   C. 4, 3, 1, 2, 5
    D. 1, 3, 5, 4, 2

1.____

2. 1. The powerlessness before private and public authorities that is the typical experience of the slum tenant is reminiscent of the situation of blue-collar workers all through the nineteenth century.
    2. Similarly, in recent years, this chapter of history has been reopened by anti-poverty groups which have attempted to organize slum tenants to enable them to bargain collectively with their landlords about the conditions of their tenancies.
    3. It is familiar history that many of the workers remedied their condition by joining together and presenting their demands collectively.
    4. Like the workers, tenants are forced by the conditions of modern life into substantial dependence on these who possess great political arid economic power.
    5. What's more, the very fact of dependence coupled with an absence of education and self-confidence makes them hesitant and unable to stand up for what they need from those in power.

    The CORRECT answer is:

    A. 5, 4, 1, 2, 3   B. 2, 3, 1, 5, 4   C. 3, 1, 5, 4, 2
    D. 1, 4, 5, 3, 2

2.____

3. 1. A railroad, for example, when not acting as a common carrier may contract; away responsibility for its own negligence.
    2. As to a landlord, however, no decision has been found relating to the legal effect of a clause shifting the statutory duty of repair to the tenant.
    3. The courts have not passed on the validity of clauses relieving the landlord of this duty and liability.
    4. They have, however, upheld the validity of exculpatory clauses in other types of contracts.
    5. Housing regulations impose a duty upon the landlord to maintain leased premises in safe condition.

3.____

6. As another example, a bailee may limit his liability except for gross negligence, willful acts, or fraud.

The CORRECT answer is:

A. 2, 1, 6, 4, 3, 5
B. 1, 3, 4, 5, 6, 2
C. 3, 5, 1, 4, 2, 6
D. 5, 3, 4, 1, 6, 2

4.
1. Since there are only samples in the building, retail or consumer sales are generally eschewed by mart occupants, and, in some instances, rigid controls are maintained to limit entrance to the mart only to those persons engaged in retailing.
2. Since World War I, in many larger cities, there has developed a new type of property, called the mart building.
3. It can, therefore, be used by wholesalers and jobbers for the display of sample merchandise.
4. This type of building is most frequently a multi-storied, finished interior property which is a cross between a retail arcade and a loft building.
5. This limitation enables the mart occupants to ship the orders from another location after the retailer or dealer makes his selection from the samples.

The CORRECT answer is:

A. 2, 4, 3, 1, 5
B. 4, 3, 5, 1, 2
C. 1, 3, 2, 4, 5
D. 1, 4, 2, 3, 5

5.
1. In general, staff-line friction reduces the distinctive contribution of staff personnel.
2. The conflicts, however, introduce an uncontrolled element into the managerial system.
3. On the other hand, the natural resistance of the line to staff innovations probably usefully restrains over-eager efforts to apply untested procedures on a large scale.
4. Under such conditions, it is difficult to know when valuable ideas are being sacrificed.
5. The relatively weak position of staff, requiring accommodation to the line, tends to restrict their ability to engage .in free, experimental innovation.

The CORRECT answer is:

A. 4, 2, 3, 1, 3
B. 1, 5, 3, 2, 4
C. 5, 3, 1, 2, 4
D. 2, 1, 4, 5, 3

KEY (CORRECT ANSWERS)

1. A
2. D
3. D
4. A
5. B

TEST 3

DIRECTIONS: Questions 1 through 4 consist of six sentences which can be arranged in a logical sequence. For each question, select the choice which places the numbered sentences in the *most logical* sequence. PRINT THE LETTER OF THE CORRECT ANSWER IN THE SPACE AT THE RIGHT.

1. 1. The burden of proof as to each issue is determined before trial and remains upon the same party throughout the trial.
    2. The jury is at liberty to believe one witness' testimony as against a number of contradictory witnesses.
    3. In a civil case, the party bearing the burden of proof is required to prove his contention by a fair preponderance of the evidence.
    4. However, it must be noted that a fair preponderance of evidence does not necessarily mean a greater number of witnesses.
    5. The burden of proof is the burden which rests upon one of the parties to an action to persuade the trier of the facts, generally the jury, that a proposition he asserts is true.
    6. If the evidence is equally balanced, or if it leaves the jury in such doubt as to be unable to decide the controversy either way, judgment must be given against the party upon whom the burden of proof rests.

    The CORRECT answer is:

    A. 3, 2, 5, 4, 1, 6   B. 1, 2, 6, 5, 3, 4   C. 3, 4, 5, 1, 2, 6
    D. 5, 1, 3, 6, 4, 2

2. 1. If a parent is without assets and is unemployed, he cannot be convicted of the crime of non-support of a child.
    2. The term "sufficient ability" has been held to mean sufficient financial ability.
    3. It does not matter if his unemployment is by choice or unavoidable circumstances.
    4. If he fails to take any steps at all, he may be liable to prosecution for endangering the welfare of a child.
    5. Under the penal law, a parent is responsible for the support of his minor child only if the parent is "of sufficient ability."
    6. An indigent parent may meet his obligation by borrowing money or by seeking aid under the provisions of the Social Welfare Law.

    The CORRECT answer is:

    A. 6, 1, 5, 3, 2, 4   B. 1, 3, 5, 2, 4, 6   C. 5, 2, 1, 3, 6, 4
    D. 1, 6, 4, 5, 2, 3

3. 1. Consider, for example, the case of a rabble rouser who urges a group of twenty people to go out and break the windows of a nearby factory.
    2. Therefore, the law fills the indicated gap with the crime of inciting to riot."
    3. A person is considered guilty of inciting to riot when he urges ten or more persons to engage in tumultuous and violent conduct of a kind likely to create public alarm.
    4. However, if he has not obtained the cooperation of at least four people, he cannot be charged with unlawful assembly.
    5. The charge of inciting to riot was added to the law to cover types of conduct which cannot be classified as either the crime of "riot" or the crime of "unlawful assembly."
    6. If he acquires the acquiescence of at least four of them, he is guilty of unlawful assembly even if the project does not materialize.

    The CORRECT answer is:

    A. 3, 5, 1, 6, 4, 2   B. 5, 1, 4, 6, 2, 3   C. 3, 4, 1, 5, 2, 6
    D. 5, 1, 4, 6, 3, 2

4. 1. If, however, the rebuttal evidence presents an issue of credibility, it is for the jury to determine whether the presumption has, in fact, been destroyed.
    2. Once sufficient evidence to the contrary is introduced, the presumption disappears from the trial.
    3. The effect of a presumption is to place the burden upon the adversary to come forward with evidence to rebut the presumption.
    4. When a presumption is overcome and ceases to exist in the case, the fact or facts which gave rise to the presumption still remain.
    5. Whether a presumption has been overcome is ordinarily a question for the court.
    6. Such information may furnish a basis for a logical inference.

    The CORRECT answer is:

    A. 4, 6, 2, 5, 1, 3   B. 3, 2, 5, 1, 4, 6   C. 5, 3, 6, 4, 2, 1
    D. 5, 4, 1, 2, 6, 3

KEY (CORRECT ANSWERS)

1. D
2. C
3. A
4. B

PREPARING WRITTEN MATERIAL

EXAMINATION SECTION
TEST 1

DIRECTIONS: Each question consists of a sentence which may or may not be an example of good English usage. Examine each sentence, considering grammar, punctuation, spelling, capitalization, and awkwardness. Then choose the correct statement about it from the four choices below it. If the English usage in the sentence given is better than any of the changes suggested in choices B, C, or D, pick choice A. (Do not pick a choice that will change the meaning of the sentence.)

1. We attended a staff conference on Wednesday the new safety and fire rules were discussed.   1.____

    A. This is an example of acceptable writing.
    B. The words "safety," "fire" and "rules" should begin with capital letters.
    C. There should be a comma after the word "Wednesday."
    D. There should be a period after the word "Wednesday" and the word "the" should begin with a capital letter

2. Neither the dictionary or the telephone directory could be found in the office library.   2.____

    A. This is an example of acceptable writing.
    B. The word "or" should be changed to "nor."
    C. The word "library" should be spelled "libery."
    D. The word "neither" should be changed to "either."

3. The report would have been typed correctly if the typist could read the draft.   3.____

    A. This is an example of acceptable writing.
    B. The word "would" should be removed.
    C. The word "have" should be inserted after the word "could."
    D. The word "correctly" should be changed to "correct."

4. The supervisor brought the reports and forms to an employees desk.   4.____

    A. This is an example of acceptable writing.
    B. The word "brought" should be changed to "took."
    C. There should be a comma after the word "reports" and a comma after the word "forms."
    D. The word "employees" should be spelled "employee's."

5. It's important for all the office personnel to submit their vacation schedules on time.   5.____

    A. This is an example of acceptable writing.
    B. The word "It's" should be spelled "Its."
    C. The word "their" should be spelled "they're."
    D. The word "personnel" should be spelled "personal."

6. The report, along with the accompanying documents, were submitted for review.   6.___

    A. This is an example of acceptable writing.
    B. The words "were submitted" should be changed to "was submitted."
    C. The word "accompanying" should be spelled "accompaning."
    D. The comma after the word "report" should be taken out.

7. If others must use your files, be certain that they understand how the system works, but insist that you do all the filing and refiling.   7.___

    A. This is an example of acceptable writing.
    B. There should be a period after the word "works," and the word "but" should start a new sentence
    C. The words "filing" and "refiling" should be spelled "fileing" and "refileing."
    D. There should be a comma after the word "but."

8. The appeal was not considered because of its late arrival.   8.___

    A. This is an example of acceptable writing.
    B. The word "its" should be changed to "it's."
    C. The word "its" should be changed to "the."
    D. The words "late arrival" should be changed to "arrival late."

9. The letter must be read carefuly to determine under which subject it should be filed.   9.___

    A. This is an example of acceptable writing.
    B. The word "under" should be changed to "at."
    C. The word "determine" should be spelled "determin."
    D. The word "carefuly" should be spelled "carefully."

10. He showed potential as an office manager, but he lacked skill in delegating work.   10.___

    A. This is an example of acceptable writing.
    B. The word "delegating" should be spelled "delagating."
    C. The word "potential" should be spelled "potencial."
    D. The words "he lacked" should be changed to "was lacking."

KEY (CORRECT ANSWERS)

1.	D	6.	B
2.	B	7.	A
3.	C	8.	A
4.	D	9.	D
5.	A	10.	A

TEST 2

DIRECTIONS: Each question consists of a sentence which may or may not be an example of good English usage. Examine each sentence, considering grammar, punctuation, spelling, capitalization, and awkwardness. Then choose the correct statement about it from the four choices below it. If the English usage in the sentence given is better than any of the changes suggested in choices B, C, or D, pick choice A. (Do not pick a choice that will change the meaning of the sentence.)

1. The supervisor wants that all staff members report to the office at 9:00 A.M. 1.____

    A. This is an example of acceptable writing.
    B. The word "that" should be removed and the word "to" should be inserted after the word "members."
    C. There should be a comma after the word "wants" and a comma after the word "office."
    D. The word "wants" should be changed to "want" and the word "shall" should be inserted after the word "members."

2. Every morning the clerk opens the office mail and distributes it . 2.____

    A. This is an example of acceptable writing.
    B. The word "opens" should be changed to "open."
    C. The word "mail" should be changed to "letters."
    D. The word "it" should be changed to "them."

3. The secretary typed more fast on a desktop computer than on a laptop computer. 3.____

    A. This is an example of acceptable writing.
    B. The words "more fast" should be changed to "faster."
    C. There should be a comma after the words "desktop computer."
    D. The word "than" should be changed to "then."

4. The new stenographer needed a desk a computer, a chair and a blotter. 4.____

    A. This is an example of acceptable writing.
    B. The word "blotter" should be spelled "blodder."
    C. The word "stenographer" should begin with a capital letter.
    D. There should be a comma after the word "desk."

5. The recruiting officer said, "There are many different goverment jobs available." 5.____

    A. This is an example of acceptable writing.
    B. The word "There" should not be capitalized.
    C. The word "goverment" should be spelled "government".
    D. The comma after the word "said" should be removed.

6. He can recommend a mechanic whose work is reliable. 6.____

    A. This is an example of acceptable writing.
    B. The word "reliable" should be spelled "relyable."
    C. The word "whose" should be spelled "who's."
    D. The word "mechanic" should be spelled "mecanic."

7. She typed quickly; like someone who had not a moment to lose. 7.___

   A. This is an example of acceptable writing.
   B. The word "not" should be removed.
   C. The semicolon should be changed to a comma.
   D. The word "quickly" should be placed before instead of after the word "typed."

8. She insisted that she had to much work to do. 8.___

   A. This is an example of acceptable writing.
   B. The word "insisted" should be spelled "incisted."
   C. The word "to" used in front of "much" should be spelled "too."
   D. The word "do" should be changed to "be done."

9. He excepted praise from his supervisor for a job well done. 9.___

   A. This is an example of acceptable writing.
   B. The word "excepted" should be spelled "accepted."
   C. The order of the words "well done" should be changed to "done well."
   D. There should be a comma after the word "supervisor."

10. What appears to be intentional errors in grammar occur several times in the passage. 10.___

    A. This is an example of acceptable writing.
    B. The word "occur" should be spelled "occurr."
    C. The word "appears" should be changed to "appear."
    D. The phrase "several times" should be changed to "from time to time."

KEY (CORRECT ANSWERS)

1.	B	6.	A
2.	A	7.	C
3.	B	8.	C
4.	D	9.	B
5.	C	10.	C

TEST 3

Questions 1-5.

DIRECTIONS: Same as for Tests 1 and 2.

1. The clerk could have completed the assignment on time if he knows where these materials were located. 1._____

    A. This is an example of acceptable writing.
    B. The word "knows" should be replaced by "had known."
    C. The word "were" should be replaced by "had been."
    D. The words "where these materials were located" should be replaced by "the location of these materials."

2. All employees should be given safety training. Not just those who have accidents. 2._____

    A. This is an example of acceptable writing.
    B. The period after the word "training" should be changed to a colon.
    C. The period after the word "training" should be changed to a semicolon, and the first letter of the word "Not" should be changed to a small "n."
    D. The period after the word "training" should be changed to a comma, and the first letter of the word "Not" should be changed to a small "n."

3. This proposal is designed to promote employee awareness of the suggestion program, to encourage employee participation in the program, and to increase the number of suggestions submitted. 3._____

    A. This is an example of acceptable writing.
    B. The word "proposal" should be spelled "preposal."
    C. The words "to increase the number of suggestions submitted" should be changed to "an increase in the number of suggestions is expected."
    D. The word "promote" should be changed to "enhance" and the word "increase" should be changed to "add to."

4. The introduction of inovative managerial techniques should be preceded by careful analysis of the specific circumstances and conditions in each department. 4._____

    A. This is an example of acceptable writing.
    B. The word "techniques" should be spelled "techneques."
    C. The word "inovative" should be spelled "innovative."
    D. A comma should be placed after the word "circumstances" and after the word "conditions."

5. This occurrence indicates that such criticism embarrasses him. 5._____

    A. This is an example of acceptable writing.
    B. The word "occurrence" should be spelled "occurence."
    C. The word "criticism" should be spelled "critisism."
    D. The word "embarrasses" should be spelled "embarases."

KEY (CORRECT ANSWERS)

1. B
2. D
3. A
4. C
5. A

ANSWER SHEET

NO. _____ PART _____ TITLE OF POSITION _____
(AS GIVEN IN EXAMINATION ANNOUNCEMENT - INCLUDE OPTION, IF ANY)

E OF EXAMINATION _____ DATE _____
(CITY OR TOWN)   (STATE)

RATING

USE THE SPECIAL PENCIL. MAKE GLOSSY BLACK MARKS.

	A B C D E		A B C D E		A B C D E		A B C D E		A B C D E
1	⋮ ⋮ ⋮ ⋮ ⋮	26	⋮ ⋮ ⋮ ⋮ ⋮	51	⋮ ⋮ ⋮ ⋮ ⋮	76	⋮ ⋮ ⋮ ⋮ ⋮	101	⋮ ⋮ ⋮ ⋮ ⋮
2	⋮ ⋮ ⋮ ⋮ ⋮	27	⋮ ⋮ ⋮ ⋮ ⋮	52	⋮ ⋮ ⋮ ⋮ ⋮	77	⋮ ⋮ ⋮ ⋮ ⋮	102	⋮ ⋮ ⋮ ⋮ ⋮
3	⋮ ⋮ ⋮ ⋮ ⋮	28	⋮ ⋮ ⋮ ⋮ ⋮	53	⋮ ⋮ ⋮ ⋮ ⋮	78	⋮ ⋮ ⋮ ⋮ ⋮	103	⋮ ⋮ ⋮ ⋮ ⋮
4	⋮ ⋮ ⋮ ⋮ ⋮	29	⋮ ⋮ ⋮ ⋮ ⋮	54	⋮ ⋮ ⋮ ⋮ ⋮	79	⋮ ⋮ ⋮ ⋮ ⋮	104	⋮ ⋮ ⋮ ⋮ ⋮
5	⋮ ⋮ ⋮ ⋮ ⋮	30	⋮ ⋮ ⋮ ⋮ ⋮	55	⋮ ⋮ ⋮ ⋮ ⋮	80	⋮ ⋮ ⋮ ⋮ ⋮	105	⋮ ⋮ ⋮ ⋮ ⋮
6	⋮ ⋮ ⋮ ⋮ ⋮	31	⋮ ⋮ ⋮ ⋮ ⋮	56	⋮ ⋮ ⋮ ⋮ ⋮	81	⋮ ⋮ ⋮ ⋮ ⋮	106	⋮ ⋮ ⋮ ⋮ ⋮
7	⋮ ⋮ ⋮ ⋮ ⋮	32	⋮ ⋮ ⋮ ⋮ ⋮	57	⋮ ⋮ ⋮ ⋮ ⋮	82	⋮ ⋮ ⋮ ⋮ ⋮	107	⋮ ⋮ ⋮ ⋮ ⋮
8	⋮ ⋮ ⋮ ⋮ ⋮	33	⋮ ⋮ ⋮ ⋮ ⋮	58	⋮ ⋮ ⋮ ⋮ ⋮	83	⋮ ⋮ ⋮ ⋮ ⋮	108	⋮ ⋮ ⋮ ⋮ ⋮
9	⋮ ⋮ ⋮ ⋮ ⋮	34	⋮ ⋮ ⋮ ⋮ ⋮	59	⋮ ⋮ ⋮ ⋮ ⋮	84	⋮ ⋮ ⋮ ⋮ ⋮	109	⋮ ⋮ ⋮ ⋮ ⋮
10	⋮ ⋮ ⋮ ⋮ ⋮	35	⋮ ⋮ ⋮ ⋮ ⋮	60	⋮ ⋮ ⋮ ⋮ ⋮	85	⋮ ⋮ ⋮ ⋮ ⋮	110	⋮ ⋮ ⋮ ⋮ ⋮

Make only ONE mark for each answer. Additional and stray marks may be counted as mistakes. In making corrections, erase errors COMPLETELY.

	A B C D E		A B C D E		A B C D E		A B C D E		A B C D E
11	⋮ ⋮ ⋮ ⋮ ⋮	36	⋮ ⋮ ⋮ ⋮ ⋮	61	⋮ ⋮ ⋮ ⋮ ⋮	86	⋮ ⋮ ⋮ ⋮ ⋮	111	⋮ ⋮ ⋮ ⋮ ⋮
12	⋮ ⋮ ⋮ ⋮ ⋮	37	⋮ ⋮ ⋮ ⋮ ⋮	62	⋮ ⋮ ⋮ ⋮ ⋮	87	⋮ ⋮ ⋮ ⋮ ⋮	112	⋮ ⋮ ⋮ ⋮ ⋮
13	⋮ ⋮ ⋮ ⋮ ⋮	38	⋮ ⋮ ⋮ ⋮ ⋮	63	⋮ ⋮ ⋮ ⋮ ⋮	88	⋮ ⋮ ⋮ ⋮ ⋮	113	⋮ ⋮ ⋮ ⋮ ⋮
14	⋮ ⋮ ⋮ ⋮ ⋮	39	⋮ ⋮ ⋮ ⋮ ⋮	64	⋮ ⋮ ⋮ ⋮ ⋮	89	⋮ ⋮ ⋮ ⋮ ⋮	114	⋮ ⋮ ⋮ ⋮ ⋮
15	⋮ ⋮ ⋮ ⋮ ⋮	40	⋮ ⋮ ⋮ ⋮ ⋮	65	⋮ ⋮ ⋮ ⋮ ⋮	90	⋮ ⋮ ⋮ ⋮ ⋮	115	⋮ ⋮ ⋮ ⋮ ⋮
16	⋮ ⋮ ⋮ ⋮ ⋮	41	⋮ ⋮ ⋮ ⋮ ⋮	66	⋮ ⋮ ⋮ ⋮ ⋮	91	⋮ ⋮ ⋮ ⋮ ⋮	116	⋮ ⋮ ⋮ ⋮ ⋮
17	⋮ ⋮ ⋮ ⋮ ⋮	42	⋮ ⋮ ⋮ ⋮ ⋮	67	⋮ ⋮ ⋮ ⋮ ⋮	92	⋮ ⋮ ⋮ ⋮ ⋮	117	⋮ ⋮ ⋮ ⋮ ⋮
18	⋮ ⋮ ⋮ ⋮ ⋮	43	⋮ ⋮ ⋮ ⋮ ⋮	68	⋮ ⋮ ⋮ ⋮ ⋮	93	⋮ ⋮ ⋮ ⋮ ⋮	118	⋮ ⋮ ⋮ ⋮ ⋮
19	⋮ ⋮ ⋮ ⋮ ⋮	44	⋮ ⋮ ⋮ ⋮ ⋮	69	⋮ ⋮ ⋮ ⋮ ⋮	94	⋮ ⋮ ⋮ ⋮ ⋮	119	⋮ ⋮ ⋮ ⋮ ⋮
20	⋮ ⋮ ⋮ ⋮ ⋮	45	⋮ ⋮ ⋮ ⋮ ⋮	70	⋮ ⋮ ⋮ ⋮ ⋮	95	⋮ ⋮ ⋮ ⋮ ⋮	120	⋮ ⋮ ⋮ ⋮ ⋮
21	⋮ ⋮ ⋮ ⋮ ⋮	46	⋮ ⋮ ⋮ ⋮ ⋮	71	⋮ ⋮ ⋮ ⋮ ⋮	96	⋮ ⋮ ⋮ ⋮ ⋮	121	⋮ ⋮ ⋮ ⋮ ⋮
22	⋮ ⋮ ⋮ ⋮ ⋮	47	⋮ ⋮ ⋮ ⋮ ⋮	72	⋮ ⋮ ⋮ ⋮ ⋮	97	⋮ ⋮ ⋮ ⋮ ⋮	122	⋮ ⋮ ⋮ ⋮ ⋮
23	⋮ ⋮ ⋮ ⋮ ⋮	48	⋮ ⋮ ⋮ ⋮ ⋮	73	⋮ ⋮ ⋮ ⋮ ⋮	98	⋮ ⋮ ⋮ ⋮ ⋮	123	⋮ ⋮ ⋮ ⋮ ⋮
24	⋮ ⋮ ⋮ ⋮ ⋮	49	⋮ ⋮ ⋮ ⋮ ⋮	74	⋮ ⋮ ⋮ ⋮ ⋮	99	⋮ ⋮ ⋮ ⋮ ⋮	124	⋮ ⋮ ⋮ ⋮ ⋮
25	⋮ ⋮ ⋮ ⋮ ⋮	50	⋮ ⋮ ⋮ ⋮ ⋮	75	⋮ ⋮ ⋮ ⋮ ⋮	100	⋮ ⋮ ⋮ ⋮ ⋮	125	⋮ ⋮ ⋮ ⋮ ⋮

ANSWER SHEET

NOV - - 2016

TEST NO. _____ PART _____ TITLE OF POSITION _____
(AS GIVEN IN EXAMINATION ANNOUNCEMENT - INCLUDE OPTION, IF ANY)

PLACE OF EXAMINATION _____ (CITY OR TOWN) _____ (STATE) _____ DATE _____

RATING

USE THE SPECIAL PENCIL. MAKE GLOSSY BLACK MARKS.

Make only ONE mark for each answer. Additional and stray marks may be counted as mistakes. In making corrections, erase errors COMPLETELY.